TV:

An Insider's Guide

How To Be A Success In The TV Industry

JULIAN DISMORE

Acknowledgements

"This book is dedicated to all the people who have taught me
stuff or helped me in my career; Debbie, Mick, John, Hugo, Duncan,
Adam, Peter, Grant, Malcolm, Pauline, James, Elliott, Sarah, Paul,
Andrew, Mark, Siobhan, Lorraine, Bob, Manoj, Miles, Jaimi, Derek,
Sean, Lorraine, Lisa, Paul, Jeremy, Simon, Sue, Irene, Tim, Sara, Sam
and many more. You know who you are!"

TV: An Insider's Guide
How To Be A Success In The TV Industry

© Julian Dismore

ISBN: 978-1-906316-65-5

Published in 2010 by HotHive Books, Evesham, UK.
www.thehothive.com

A CIP record of this book is available from the British Library.

Printed in the UK by TJ International, Padstow

About The Author

Julian Dismore is an award-winning TV series director and web video producer. He is also an international TV format consultant and experienced media skills trainer.

Julian has produced top-rating programmes for ITV, Channel 4, Five, Sky, Discovery, National Geographic and Animal Planet. He has been series producer and director on dozens of highly-regarded programmes.

His credits include *Crash Scene Investigators* (ITV), *Missing Mums* (Sky One), *Stunt School* (Five and Discovery), *O'Shea's Dangerous Reptiles* (Channel 4 and Animal Planet), *Mistresses* (ITV), *Trisha Goddard* (Five), *Jimmy's* (ITV), *Game Rangers: South Africa* (National Geographic), *First Tuesday* (ITV), *New Boy* (Channel 4), *Holidays from Hell* (ITV), *3D* (ITV), *Skin Deep* (Discovery and ITV), *Missing Children: Lorraine Kelly Investigates* (Sky), *Mr Right* (ITV), *Network First* (ITV) and *Britain's Psychic Challenge* (Five).

Julian is highly experienced in the following programme areas: police, medical, wildlife, current affairs, factual entertainment and documentaries. He also self-shoots and edits corporate films, specialising in web videos and sports DVDs. Julian has set up and produced YouTube channels for a number of clients, including the Rajasthan Royals cricket team, winners of the inaugural Indian Premier League.

Julian has delivered training in TV production and web video presenting skills to students and experienced TV professionals for many years. He has a strong track record of helping people to get their first break in TV, and then excelling in their jobs once they have their foot on the ladder.

Julian's TV career has been an emotional rollercoaster, including falling off Krakatoa, posing as an undercover paedophile in the Far East, being bitten by a king cobra, winning a 'dance off' with LA gang members and losing a high-speed car chase with Vinnie Jones down the M1.

He is more aware than anyone how eventful, exciting and unpredictable a career in television can be – and he is passionate about helping others in the TV industry to achieve their potential.

To find out more about Julian's TV training and web video courses, email: directtvtraining@yahoo.co.uk.

Contents

ON AIR

Foreword:
Lorraine Kelly

Lorraine Kelly
TV Presenter

Foreword

The world of broadcasting has changed enormously since Julian and I first started making programmes. Crews have got smaller, schedules tighter and budgets have shrunk. But one thing has stayed the same: television is the best career there is.

No other job gives you access to people's lives, opportunities to travel the world and the chance to tell fascinating stories to millions of people. But because it's such a great career, it's very hard to get into. Demand for TV jobs far exceeds supply and when you have a coveted job in broadcasting, it's harder than ever these days to progress up the career ladder. It's a real cut-throat business with thousands of people competing for the best jobs.

That's why this book is a must read for anyone who wants to get into TV, and it's essential reading for anyone already in TV who wants to be better at their job.

Julian has worked in the TV industry for well over 20 years in pretty much every role. He's been a runner, researcher, associate producer, edit producer, producer/director, series producer and an executive. He has worked on staff for big ITV companies and small indies and also as a freelancer. He can shoot and edit his own material, produces corporate DVDs and web videos and has been running TV training courses for many years.

Julian has vast experience hiring people for a wide variety of TV productions – so he knows all about what it takes to get into TV. He has worked his way up the TV career ladder and is multi-skilled, so he can give solid advice on each role. As a freelancer he has had to apply for his fair share of jobs himself, so he's well aware how tough it can be securing the best jobs, and the techniques required to excel at them.

Having worked with Julian on numerous productions, I can testify that he's not only a joy to work with but he's organised, utterly professional and able to think on his feet. He's cool under pressure and full of passion for the projects he undertakes. Above all, he's a grafter who knows that the harder you work in TV, strangely, the luckier you get! He has buckets of common sense and is full of practical advice. When you combine that with his creative flair you have an incredible combination. Listen to this man!

I hope you enjoy his book – and good luck achieving your ambitions!

Introduction:
You Mad?

Introduction: You Mad?

A lot of offices in the 'real world' have a notice that says: 'You don't have to be mad to work here – but it helps!' Well, that doesn't apply to the world of TV – you do have to be mad. Gone are the days when job security, paid holidays, final salary pensions and in-house training were the norm in the TV industry. Now it's usually short-term contracts, long hours, low pay and lots of stress – and that's when you've had a good year. However, despite all this, TV is still the best job in the world.

If you're a curious person who likes to find out what makes people tick, an adventurous person who enjoys a challenge and a creative person who loves making something for others to enjoy, then TV is right up your street – and it's a guaranteed anecdote-fest. You'll definitely not be short of a tale or two to tell your grandchildren when you hang up your filming boots.

To prove it, here's a quiz.

There are 13 statements about my career below: 12 are true, and one is a lie. Can you work out which one is the lie? (While you do that, just imagine how few anecdotes I'd have if I'd followed my godfather's advice and become an accountant.) I've...

1. fallen 30 feet off the Krakatoa volcano in the middle of the night
2. kissed an HIV-positive prostitute, a flea-ridden camel and Robbie Coltrane
3. filmed undercover pretending to be a paedophile in sex bars in the Far East
4. shot a Hollywood icon, a porn star and a stuntman with his head up a horse's bum
5. starred as Captain Hook on an ITV cookery series and as a pundit on Ukraine TV
6. been bitten by a king cobra in a snake charming village in India
7. defied government advice and flown into a war zone to film cricket web videos
8. been abducted in the South African jungle late at night by an ex-British spy
9. eaten testicles, cleaned up dog dirt and donated sperm, all in the line of duty
10. been involved in a high-speed car chase with Vinnie Jones on the M1
11. run out of outboard motor fuel on a crocodile and hippo-infested lagoon
12. danced with midgets in Russia, gang members in LA and tribesmen in the Bush
13. broken the law in Texas – there's still a warrant out for my arrest.

Which is the lie? Unlucky number 13. The police are actually after me in Utah!

If you'd like to see some pictures taken during my various adventures around the world, feel free to flick to the centre pages. You'll be disappointed to hear that certain photos haven't made it for taste and decency reasons, namely me donating sperm, eating testicles, dancing with a midget and kissing a prostitute with HIV. (What a night that was.)

So without further ado, let me talk you through this book. I'm about to give you hundreds of insider's tips on how to get into TV, and how to get on if you're already in the industry. This is all from my perspective and I definitely don't have all the answers, but having worked in TV for more than two decades, I do know quite a few tricks of the trade.

From personal experience I know that you need to be very good at your job to survive in the cut-throat world of TV. You also need to be able to work in a team. It helps enormously if you understand what everyone else on your team is doing and why they're doing it. This book may answer questions about your colleagues' roles that you've been afraid to ask.

In an increasingly multi-skilled industry it pays to be proficient in other areas. If you can shoot your own material, record your own sound and set up your own shoots, it might give you the edge when a promotion or better job opportunity comes up. This book explains all of this and more.

So, fasten your seatbelts and set your sat nav for an emotional rollercoaster ride to an exciting future (as we say in TV) – this book could change your life!

One thing you will notice throughout this book is that I have tended to use 'he' rather than 'she' or 'he/she'. This is despite many of the top people in TV being female. It is just quicker to write (and read) if we stick to the masculine gender. You will also find other gender-specific terminology, such as 'cameraman', used regularly. This is just a phrase used in the media – it doesn't mean cameramen can't be women!

Chapter 1:
The Secret To TV Success

Chapter 1: The Secret To TV Success

Before we get into the nuts and bolts of each individual role, let me fill you in on the secret of a successful career in TV. You need to be good at pretty much everything: multi-skilling is the order of the day. If you're looking to work in TV, you should read all the chapters in this book, whatever you want to be when you grow up.

And if you're already a researcher, shooting associate producer or producer/director, you should also read this book from cover to cover. It's good to have as many skills in your locker as possible. Plus it helps if you know what everyone else on your team is supposed to be doing, and how it can be done well. Sometimes, if a job's worth doing, you need to be able to do it yourself.

To forewarn you, some skills that apply to your particular role may be in another section. Interviewing people on camera is discussed in Chapter 9 (How To Be A Presenter), but those skills are also helpful to anyone whose job it is to ask questions: researchers, shooting associate producers, producers, etc. So read the whole book – you won't regret it!

Just to give you some background, all this multi-skilling is relatively recent. When I first started in TV, people had strict roles. I was a programme researcher: that was my job and that was it. If I had picked up a camera and started using it, there would have been serious issues – I might even have been fired. There was strict demarcation between jobs and roles. It would take ages to get a 'director's ticket' or become an official cameraman – and those positions were guarded fiercely. How things have changed – and to prove the point, let me tell you a story about what happened to me a few years ago.

Web videos from a war zone

In November 2008 I was flying to Mumbai to film a DVD about the Rajasthan Royals Indian Premier League (IPL) cricket team during the Champions League tournament. I had my own Sony Z1 camera and was looking forward to filming superstars of the game such as Shane Warne and Graeme Smith. When I got to Heathrow, I saw on the news that a terrorist incident had started in Mumbai and there were numerous casualties. I didn't contemplate not going: Mumbai is a big place, and I was confident I'd be fine.

When I arrived, I realised I had flown into a war zone. As I left the airport there were dozens of taxi drivers holding up worrying signs: 'CNN War Correspondent', 'BBC News', etc. It's never a good sign being on the same plane as Kate Adie.

My taxi driver whisked me through various army checkpoints to my hotel which, as fortune would have it, was the third best hotel in Mumbai. The top two were still being attacked and under a state of siege. I was told by the frightened hotel staff to stay in my room and lock the door, as we could be next to be attacked.

Lying in the foetal position sucking my thumb on my bed got a bit tedious after a while, so I decided to get some work done. I got the cricketers who also were under hotel arrest to come to my room, where I interviewed them with my Z1 camera. I then edited the interviews using Adobe Premiere on my laptop and uploaded them to YouTube. I set up a new site – 'Rajasthan Royals TV' – which immediately started to get hits.

A decade or so earlier, this would have been impossible for a variety of technical and practical reasons: you would have needed a whole building to film, edit and broadcast a programme, and very few people were allowed to shoot, cut and produce their own material. And the idea of setting up a new channel? Not possible without government legislation and lot of red tape.

However, such multi-skilling is increasingly expected these days. There are very few 'pure' researchers or directors around. Shooting associate producers (who can film their own material) and 'predators' (producer/editors who can cut their own programmes) are the order of the day. It can be hard work doing several jobs at once and quality usually suffers: 'Jack of all trades rather than master of one', and so on. But this is the way the industry is going, and you need to adapt to survive.

Plus it can be great fun making something all on your own. As web videos become the main way of broadcasting video content, 'do-it-yourself TV' will become par for the course. There will be more TV jobs out there, but they will be very different to the ones that people jostled for when I first started. Also, with in-house training being so rare, you'll need to acquire the requisite skills yourself – which is one of the reasons why I've written this book.

It is impossible to totally skill you up in 50,000 words or so, but we can make a start. Are you ready? Let's rock and roll!

Chapter 2:
How To Get Into TV

Chapter 2: How To Get Into TV

From time to time in this book I'll throw in personal stories for the purposes of illustration – and this one is about how I got my first job in TV. It was a researcher position in the Science Department at Yorkshire TV (YTV) in Leeds.

Basically, I broke almost every rule, so don't do what I did. I only wrote a few letters to potential employers rather than hundreds. I got invited for an interview but wrote down the wrong address, so I turned up late. I wore a suit because I thought you were supposed to for interviews – the interviewer was wearing jeans and a T-shirt. Because I was late I thought I'd blown it, so I relaxed, sat back (appalling body language) and told a few anecdotes about my summer in the USA. Incredibly, I beat the other 85 Oxbridge candidates who applied for the job and was hired – partly because I came from the seaside resort of Bridlington and my future boss liked to go there for holidays, but mainly due to the fact that my relaxed approach set me apart from the rest.

I wouldn't recommend this interview technique, and the tips later in this chapter will give you much better strategies, but there is one thing you must remember. You will face stiff competition getting into TV, and even stiffer competition getting the best jobs as you progress up the career ladder, so it's important that you stand out from the crowd. The best way to do this is to be yourself, work hard and be passionate about what you do. If you care about your programme, the viewers will too.

(Incidentally, whenever I say 'TV' in this book, I mean conventional TV – BBC, ITV, Sky, etc, as well as video journalism and web videos – which are the future.)

Getting started in TV: contacts, emails and networking

CONTACTS

The saying goes, 'It's not what you know, it's who you know'. Well, it's both in TV – but who you know is particularly important. Personal contacts can help you get your first job and they can help you get better jobs after that. So how do you make the most out of your contacts? Well, the first challenge is finding them…

SOURCING CONTACTS: FIVE TOP TIPS

1. **Be alert!**
    Contacts are all around you. If you are a student and have any sense, you'll be heavily involved in a university TV society, hospital radio station or student newspaper. It is likely that one of your peers has been able to secure some work experience, so ask your

contact for their contact. But make sure you repay the favour at a later stage – it's all about keeping your sources sweet.

2. Spread your net wide

Normally someone you know knows someone. Your mum's hairdresser's cousin's friend is a potential contact – if they work in TV. So is someone in TV who went to your college, university or school at some point in the last 50 years.

3. Watch the credits on the programmes you like

Watch programme credits and keep an eye out for the following people: the producer, series producer and production manager. These are potential contacts, but you need to watch out for the name of the company at the end of the credits, so that you can track them down using tip number 4.

4. Use the internet and be a detective

All the major TV programme-making companies have easy to find websites. The potential contacts from tip number 3 may be on there. The website is also likely to have a recruitment or work experience email address on the homepage. Send in your CV – just don't hold your breath waiting for an answer.

5. Read trade papers and magazines such as *Broadcast*

The articles will feature the key players in the industry. In addition, there will be stories about companies which have just got programme commissions and may need staff. Once you have names and companies, you have all the info you need. It's email time!

EMAILING CONTACTS: SEVEN TOP TIPS

1. Finding their address

The email address of your potential contact is probably:

- firstname.secondname@companyname.tv or
- initial.secondname@companyname.co.uk

It won't take Sherlock Holmes to work out their email address from the company website. Alternatively, try all the permutations, as one should get through; however, that brings the next challenge…

2. What to write?

The key principle to apply here is the 'golden rule' of Direct TV Training (one of my companies): 'Put yourself in the other person's shoes' – whether it's the person watching your TV show, the person receiving your programme idea or, in this case, the person reading your email. In all likelihood they'll be busy, stressed and tired, because that is the world of TV. They'll want to read an email that is succinct, impressive and clear.

So, your introductory email should be short and to the point: 'I'm writing to apply for work experience and here are some reasons why you should give me a chance...'

3. **Remember: it's a TV company, not a charity**

They are not going to want to waste valuable time and energy training you up from scratch: they'll want you to be productive from Day 1. Your email needs to establish that you already have some useful skills.

4. **Keep it relevant**

Your GCSE in needlework is irrelevant, as is the fact you are captain of the university rugby team or president of the ballroom dancing club. What they want to know is what relevant experience you have. If you have done some student TV you must include it, although I would suggest you call it 'Youth TV'. Are you a YouTube video producer? Anyone can do it these days, but it still shows that you are genuinely interested in the media. Previous work experience? This is worth its weight in gold – you can't be hopeless if someone else has given you a chance.

5. **Try to get 'face time'**

Don't forget to include the line: 'If you're not looking for someone at the moment, please can I still come and ask your advice on how to get into TV?' It's all about meeting people face-to-face. Once you are in the building and they see what a wonderful human being you are, you'd be surprised how often something crops up.

6. **Use forwarding to your advantage**

Always end your email with: 'If you don't have any work experience positions available, please can you forward this email to anyone you know who has?' TV people love to forward emails to other TV people to deal with – and you never know, the other person may be looking for someone just like you.

7. **Attach your CV**

More about CVs over the page.

NETWORKING: SEVEN TOP TIPS

1. **Follow up with a phone call**

Just sending out an email or two isn't enough. You have to remember that you are not the centre of their world. It's highly likely that your email has been deleted or put into a folder that Indiana Jones would struggle to locate. Always follow up with a phone call: 'I sent an email last week, I'm just checking it arrived okay...' In other words, do a bit of phone networking. There is no point being shy if you're after a job in TV.

2. **Give your contacts network the chance to grow**

It's extremely important that you send hundreds and hundreds of emails. The more seeds you sow, the more chance you've got of one arriving in an inbox at just the right moment. If a producer has just been let down by that week's work experience person and needs someone else quick, you could be in business.

3. **Organise your contacts list**
    What is the point of finding all these valuable contacts if you don't keep track of their email addresses and phone numbers? Keep organised and back up all the information. You never know when you might need them.

4. **Group your contacts in your email account**
    Have groups of contacts in your email library. For example, 'Jobsearch contacts' or 'Work experience contacts'. As this builds (hopefully) you can email them all at once, the next time you come available. I would suggest that you email your message to yourself and blind copy (bcc) your list – ask a friend if you don't know what that is. Doing it this way means they won't get all the other contact email addresses and feel a bit less special as a result.

5. **If you do get a work experience opportunity, make sure you do a great job!**
    It goes without saying that if you get a coveted work experience position, you need to do a brilliant job. (More information about how to do this can be found in Chapter 4.)

6. **Do some face-to-face networking**
    Work experience is a valuable opportunity to make more contacts. Network yourself senseless: go for drinks after work, make cups of tea for everyone and pick people's brains during breaks.

7. **Leave on a good note**
    I recall one work experience person sending an email to the whole company on her last day: 'Thanks for all your help, there's a big box of chocolates in reception.' Shrewd move: her email address was in everyone's inbox, and on a subliminal level they associated her with chocolate. Nice.

CV writing: how to sell yourself

Your CV is a selling document and, like any product, it needs to be geared to the buyer. Again, apply the 'Golden Rule': imagine you're the person reading it. Pretend you're a stressed-out producer looking for a work experience person late at night because you've been let down by the person you've had lined up for months.

Do you want to be trying to read a CV with small barely legible font? Do you want lots of irrelevant detail about GCSEs? Are you interested in academic referees who will wax lyrical about dissertations analysing gecko droppings in Mongolia? In the words of the late, great comedian Frankie Howerd, 'Nay, nay and thrice nay'.

WRITING YOUR CV: 12 TOP TIPS

1. **Layout**

   Everyone loves nice layouts. Lists are good. Are you enjoying this one? Of course you are. It means that you can scan a document quicker – and in TV, quick is good.

2. **Font**

   I'd suggest Arial 12 point, but this is your call. Just make sure that it doesn't strain the eyesight of a weary old TV professional.

3. **Contact information – what to include**

   At the top, do put your name (no middle names, they're not necessary), email address and mobile phone number with a space in the middle. The space makes it easier to read. (Don't bother with your home landline. You don't want your mum to answer the call, do you?)

4. **What not to include**

   At the top, don't put your age (why rub it in that you're so young with your whole life ahead of you? It will just make the reader feel envious). Also, don't put your home address – they're not going to write you a letter. Why let them know that you live hundreds of miles away from where the work experience opportunity is located? They probably won't bother to call you and you won't get the chance to persuade them that you're happy to travel to the end of the world to get your big chance in TV.

5. **Your email address matters**

   Academic addresses flag up that you're a student and the address will soon become obsolete, so get a hotmail, Yahoo! or gmail address. It needs your first name at the front, so if they remember your name, it will come up quicker in their email library. Also, it needs to be sensible. Recently, I saw 'whatsyourproblem@etc' – it did not indicate an accommodating employee!

6. **Keep the content of your CV relevant**

   The reader wants to know that you are genuinely interested in TV: your CV must back that up. At the top needs to be relevant work experience or jobs, then relevant training, then relevant university clubs or societies, etc. (You may spot a theme here: the word 'relevant'.)

7. **Delete irrelevant stuff**

   Your GCSEs were useful at the time because they helped you move on to the next stage of your education. They aren't relevant now. Neither are most of your university clubs or hobbies. If you can't relate them to TV in some way, don't waste valuable space on them. It goes without saying that you need to make the most out of your precious university time and do media-related activities. You'll regret it if you don't.

8. **Spell it right**

   I once had a CV which had 'Curriculum Vitae' at the top. A bit daft, it's obvious what it is! What's more, they had spelt it wrong! It made me laugh – before I chucked it in the bin. TV is all about detail: imagine misspelling a presenter's name or getting a crucial phone number wrong on a call sheet.

9. **'Finesse' your CV, but don't invent things!**

   For example, if you've done one article for the university newspaper, put down student journalism. If you've done one intern day for a TV company, put down work experience and the company. Don't flag up that it was just for one day: this is what I call 'finessing the truth'. However, if you totally invent things, you will get caught out.

10. **Referees are crucial**

    TV people want to hear what other TV people think about you. That is why you need to get some work experience in a TV company and make a good enough impression to get a reference out of it. Failing that, at least have a referee in the big wide world. I would never call an academic for a reference – their experience of you is too different from what I would want from you.

11. **Make your interests interesting!**

    This is your chance to emphasise that you're a TV person through and through, and you have a genuinely fascinating life that I may want to meet you to talk about. Anyone who puts 'reading' and 'travel' on their CV should be shot for lack of imagination. If travel really is your hobby, take a camcorder with you and film some web videos while you're abroad. If you do like to read, track down and interview your favourite author and put it on YouTube (assuming that they're not under house arrest in Burma).

12. **Ignore people who say it all has to be on one page**

    If you have lots of fantastic stuff to put on your CV, don't feel constrained to one page. But do keep it brief overall – you don't want to send a busy TV executive a novel.

Interview technique: before, during and after

So, you've fired off hundreds of speculative emails. You've probably heard nothing in reply. You've followed up with dozens of phone calls and been fobbed off by busy secretaries every time. You've finessed and improved your CV regularly and begun to despair – but then, out of the blue, you get a call from a TV company inviting you in 'for a chat'.

Please note, there's no such thing as a 'chat' in TV. This is an interview which could get you into television and change your life. Please also note, if you get a call like this, you must take it – whatever you're doing. Once I called someone to invite them in for a 'chat' and they asked me to call back because they were having lunch. Obviously I called the next person on the list.

That person took my call, came in, got the position and now they're head of the BBC. (Not really – but you get the point.)

When you get the call from a production company, it'll say 'Number Withheld'. Try to get the phone number, name and company of the person who has called you. If they forget to call you back, you have the information you need to chase them, plus a new contact for your contacts list. Below you'll find some tips on how to do well in interviews. The tips are not just for work experience interviews; many of my suggestions apply to interviews for a wide variety of roles: from researcher to assistant producer to producer. It is quite a big section because if you're to progress rapidly in TV you'll go to dozens of interviews in your career. (In fact, I'm going to one this evening. Wish me luck!)

BEFORE THE INTERVIEW: EIGHT TOP TIPS

1. **Anticipate the obvious questions and prepare your answers**

   There are some questions you will almost certainly be asked:

   Why should we hire you?
   What can you bring to this job?
   Which of our programmes have you seen?
   What did you think to them?
   Talk me through your CV.
   What training have you had?

   Jot down what your answers will be if they do come up. Writing things down makes them easier to remember.

2. **Research the company**
   It is essential that you know something about the company's productions, key staff and latest commissions. They're bound to ask you about them to check that you've made the effort.

3. **Find out who you are meeting**
   Look into their career so you can talk about how much you enjoyed a show they've made. Everyone in TV likes having their ego massaged! And you may have a mutual friend who worked on that show. The interviewer won't want them to know that they didn't give you a job!

4. **Research the role for which you are applying**
   A runner position on a drama is very different to a runner position on a cookery show, which is very different to a runner position on a quiz show. You need a good idea of what you'll be doing in order to be able to convince your interviewer that you'll be able to do it. (There is more information on runner roles in chapter 4 on page 36.)

5. **Watch the programme you are applying to work on**
   Now that BBC iPlayer and other 'watch again' sites are on the internet, doing this should be easy. If the programme isn't anywhere on the internet, call the company and ask them to send some DVDs. They probably won't have time, but you'll get brownie points for asking.

6. **Rehearse the interview with a friend**
   Get a friend to run through the obvious questions with you. This role-play may feel a bit foolish, but it will get your brain working. Ask your friend for constructive feedback. Did you waffle and shuffle in your seat? What was your body language like? Asking a friend's advice is a sign of strength, not weakness.

7. **Check your chest**
   Ask your friend if the top of your chest or middle of your neck went bright red when the pressure was on – it often does, especially with women, and can distract the interviewer. If you have redness issues, wear something to hide it.

8. **Don't dress too smartly or too scruffily**
   A suit and tie isn't right for a TV interview, but being too scruffy shows a lack of respect and common sense. One interviewee of mine came in ripped jeans and a T-shirt and had piercings from head to toe. The research job involved going to meet well-to-do landowners. What would they have thought of him? He didn't get the job.

DURING THE INTERVIEW: 15 TOP TIPS

1. **First impressions are important**
   Your handshake should be firm, but not bone-crushing. A weak handshake reflects a weak character. (I think Confucius said that.)

2. **Don't say anything bad about programmes made by the company**
   Their programmes are their babies. You wouldn't criticise their babies, would you? Would you? What kind of a monster are you?!

3. **Rehearse some professional sounding chat about their shows**
   Say that you like them and use terms that sound professional: 'Nicely paced', 'Good choice of music', 'Real sense of jeopardy', etc. This also applies to introductory emails. Use grown up language. If you say 'I love your programmes' you will sound about eight years old. Finally, never pretend that you have seen a programme when you haven't. You'll be found out immediately.

4. **Talk positively about your last boss**
   That boss you hated could be the interviewer's best friend. And if you slag off your last boss, the interviewer might think that you'll do the same about him when you leave this job.

5. Take your CV and a couple of copies with you

You will probably be asked to talk through your CV. Enjoy it: what's better than talking about yourself? Bring copies along – the interviewer may be so impressed that they invite in their boss to meet you.

6. Don't be scared of silence

During an interview there can be awkward pauses. If this happens, the best strategy is not to be intimidated. Some interviewers deliberately use silence to see how you respond under stress.

7. Body language is important

Yours should be attentive and slightly leaning forward. Don't come across as too laid-back and relaxed, it may look like you aren't bothered.

8. Adopt the right tone

Don't sound too full of yourself. Remember, your position on the TV 'food chain' is lower than low (for the time being)!

9. Don't fidget

Playing with your hair, clicking pen tops or unconsciously touching parts of the body is distracting for the interviewer.

10. Have 'banker answers'

These are answers that you want to shoehorn into the interview somewhere because they make you look good. Perhaps you want to name drop the companies where you have worked? Have you done a training course that might impress them? Or filmed YouTube videos on a canoe while floating down the Amazon? There's nothing worse than leaving an interview and thinking, 'I wish I'd said that'. (Well, I suppose being waterboarded by the CIA is worse, but even BBC interviews aren't that bad.)

11. Be enthusiastic all the way through

If you don't show that you're super keen, you haven't got a chance.

12. Avoid flagging towards the end

Watch out for this, especially if it is your first interview for a while and you're out of mental shape. Another reason for a rigorous role-play beforehand to sharpen you up.

13. Always have a question at the end

As the interview draws to a close, you're likely to be asked if you have any questions. Don't say 'What is the pay?' It sounds like money is all you're bothered about. Do say something sensible: perhaps enquire about other productions that the company has coming up, or use this opportunity to shoehorn in your banker answer, eg 'I recently did work experience at the BBC which involved checking scripts and taking photos of locations. Will those skills help in this role?'

14. **Politely ask when you will hear their decision**

   You don't want to be on tenterhooks weeks after they've informed the successful candidate.

15. **End on a positive note**

   You could reiterate how keen you are to work for them and what you feel you could bring to the job.

AFTER THE INTERVIEW: FIVE TOP TIPS

1. **Don't leave it too long before finding out the state of play**

   After a few days, call and ask if there is any news: perhaps politely point out that another job you're applying for needs a reply. 'I really like your job, but I'm being pressed to make a decision. Can you give me a steer on how it's looking?'

2. **Charm the secretary**

   They may give you an indication of your chances of success, even if nothing is official yet. This tactic helped me get my first job. I almost became a market researcher because I was strapped for cash, but the head of department's PA told me, off the record, that I'd got the job. They were just waiting for the unions to clear it – it was a different world then!

3. **If you don't get it, don't worry about it**

   Treat it as a learning experience.

4. **Don't by shy about asking why**

   No employer will take offence if you ring up and politely ask how you could have strengthened your application, or what experience they felt you were missing. If you can absorb constructive criticism without getting upset, you'll be able to use the feedback for next time.

5. **Try to get another interview ASAP**

   The sooner you're back in the saddle, the better. The more interviews you go to, the better you'll get.

Interviews: some classic questions

WHAT'S YOUR GREATEST WEAKNESS?

Think of an answer which is actually a disguised strength. For example:

'Sometimes I get so committed to a programme that I work much too hard, even at the expense of my social life. It can become seven days a week for me when I really get into a project.'

The interviewer will probably smile, realise you've avoided the trap and move on. Whatever you do, avoid revealing real weaknesses:

'Actually I'm habitually late, dishonest and shirk responsibility whenever and wherever I can!'

WHAT IS YOUR WEEKLY RATE?

If this is a paid position, don't waffle – come out with your rate straight away. Runners normally get something between £100 and £300 per week. Add a few pounds to your last weekly rate, but keep it sensible – you're not Martin Scorsese – yet.

ARE YOU GOING FOR ANY OTHER JOBS AT THE MOMENT?

Don't say, 'No, there's nothing else in the pipeline.' It makes you sound desperate – and a bit sad. Always give the impression that you have a few irons in the fire. If they think you are in demand, your desirability will increase. Put yourself in their position: they want to fill the position as painlessly and effectively as possible, so if they think you're about to get snaffled up by someone else, they'll realise they need to move fast to get you. However make sure you add, 'But this is the job I really want'.

Postscript: practise makes perfect!

There's no doubt that being interviewed isn't to everyone's taste. However, the more you do it and the better you prepare, the better you'll become. Hopefully it will get to the point where you enjoy the cut and thrust of interviews. As with most things, practise makes perfect. Well, almost!

Chapter 3:
Different Roles In TV

Chapter 3: Different Roles In TV

There are many jobs in TV, and this chapter gives brief job descriptions of some of them. There are two reasons I list these for you. One is so that you have a full overview of most of the possible career options available to you. The other is to add to your industry knowledge. If you're a runner in your first job and you're asked to go and help the first assistant director, it helps if you know what they do. You're less likely to make a fool of yourself!

On a similar note, if you're sent for a 'long stand', it might be worth smiling sweetly and replying, 'Shall I get some "invisible paint" while I'm at it?' You'll have passed your first initiative test!

I've broken the list down into factual, drama and studio programmes. By the way, these are just some of the many roles in these areas (apologies if I've missed yours out). There are also crossover roles in these different genres, so bear this in mind too.

Factual programmes: production team roles

CAMERAMAN

The cameraman films the footage on a big heavy camera. He or she needs to have good stamina and the patience of a saint. A saint with strong shoulders…

SOUND RECORDIST

Sound recordists work to ensure that the highest quality sound is recorded during filming. They know good jokes and are usually called Simon or Simone. They occasionally fall asleep and snore loudly during interviews.

PRODUCTION COORDINATOR

The production coordinator works closely with the production manager to ensure that all the necessary paperwork is generated and distributed, hotel and transport arrangements are made, equipment is booked, etc.

PRODUCTION MANAGER

Production managers work closely with the production accountant to ensure that the production gets made on time and on budget. They should be calm and patient. Shoots are like weddings – something always goes wrong.

RUNNER

Runners are expected to do whatever they are asked (within reason), quickly and efficiently, such as making tea, buying papers, photocopying, fetching tapes, etc. Enthusiasm, stamina and initiative are vital traits.

RESEARCHER

The researcher finds people, stories and locations. They are an invaluable member of the team. They must be well motivated and a constant source of ideas. Excellent communication skills are required (and good jokes).

SHOOTING ASSOCIATE PRODUCER (AKA ASSISTANT PRODUCER)

The shooting associate producer is able to do the researcher role proficiently and operate a camera too. They need directing skills so that they can step in and direct the crew if the producer/director is unavailable.

DUBBING MIXER

The dubbing mixer works on the final sound mix of the programme. They build layers of audio, using the sound recorded on location, commentary, library material (eg wind effects) and music. Then they mix it all together for the producer/director to sign off.

GRAPHIC DESIGNER

The graphic designer produces the programmes graphics. These include title sequences, 'bumpers' (the logos that open and close the parts in the programme), end credits and sometimes programme content, such as maps. They play a big role in certain genres, for example science programmes such as *Horizon*.

EDITOR

The editor uses sophisticated edit systems such as Avid and Final Cut to cut the programme and help the producer/director achieve their vision. You must be creative, visual and tolerant to be an editor. Patience is a virtue – you spend a lot of time in confined spaces with producer/directors!

DIRECTOR

The director is in charge of the creative look of a production. With a big crew it's like being a conductor, ensuring that everyone in the team is playing the same tune. The director needs to be a visual genius and able to withstand intense pressure.

PRODUCER

The producer is responsible for the content of the show. In factual programmes the producer often directs as well, so the producer/director is responsible for the content and look of the show. (More on the producer/director role in chapter 8.)

Please note: as budgets come down, factual programmes are increasingly being made with much smaller teams than this!

Drama: production team roles

FIRST ASSISTANT DIRECTOR

This first assistant director makes sure that the filming is on schedule. They must be authoritative but not rude; bossy but not annoying.

SECOND ASSISTANT DIRECTOR

The second assistant director is responsible for finding extras and organising the daily call sheet. The call sheet has details of who needs to be on set and at what time, transport arrangements, extras required, contact details, etc.

THIRD ASSISTANT DIRECTOR

The third assistant director makes sure actors are in make-up and wardrobe at the right time and on set when needed. Third assistant directors also ensure that the artists are well looked after. They need to be able to 'keep people sweet'.

BEST BOY

This is a senior electrician. He needs to be able to communicate with the other electricians and the creatives. It's only in this list because everyone always asks what a 'Best Boy' does!

CAMERAMAN

Some directors of photography don't physically operate the camera. They are busy checking light levels and liaising with the director until the last minute before the camera rolls, thus requiring an experienced camera operator.

COSTUME DESIGNER

The costume designer is responsible for providing appropriate costumes and accessories within strict budget constraints. They take into account the period of the drama and the characters of the actors for whom they're providing clothes.

PRODUCTION DESIGNER

The production designer is in charge of the visual look of sets and locations. A design background is essential, as well as strong visual awareness. He may be responsible for a large design budget, so financial skills are also required.

SCRIPTWRITER

The writer may come up with the original idea for a TV programme or be commissioned to write a screenplay from an existing concept. Writers must be able to work to deadlines and be willing to endure a long hard slog for work.

DIRECTOR OF PHOTOGRAPHY

The director of photography works in close partnership with the director to ensure that their visual ideas are realised. The director of photography needs to work effectively with the gaffer (chief electrician) on the lighting and the cameraman on the shots.

LOCATION MANAGER

The location manager finds locations and makes sure that they are left in a satisfactory condition. They must be persuasive when it comes to getting the location that the director has set their heart on – at a reasonable price.

These shows include many of the roles listed above, plus the following:

VISION MIXER

The vision mixer works with the director in the gallery to select which shots to use from a number of sources (eg multi-camera shoots). They must be able to cope with pressure and directors who shout!

FLOOR MANAGER

The floor manager coordinates and manages everything that happens on the studio floor during a rehearsal or production, including cueing actors, sorting props and overseeing an audience. They need to be calm and authoritative.

PRODUCTION ASSISTANT

The production assistant provides vital administrative support: organising scripts, call sheets and daily reports as well as booking hotels, hiring equipment and sorting out travel arrangements, etc. Their role is similar to the production coordinator in factual programmes.

Those are the headlines on just some of the roles in TV. The rest of this book focuses on the main roles in factual programmes and how to be good at them. For me, factual programmes are the best to work on. Real people, real locations, real stories and more foreign trips!

Remember, the harder you work and the better you do, the more you will be able to pick and choose your jobs. You'll earn more and progress faster, so pay attention!

Chapter 4:
Early TV Roles And
Essential Skills

I was lucky enough to start out as a researcher making network TV programmes. Within a year I was producing them. It was pretty rare then (late 1980s); it's unheard of now. Most people go through long, unofficial apprenticeships doing unpaid work experience as a runner, edit assistant or production coordinator before they get a sniff of a researcher position.

This can go on for months. There have been industry initiatives to clamp down on what is seen as exploitation of unpaid staff, and no doubt there have been abuses of the system. Many young people are desperate to get into TV and are willing to work long hours for nothing. Producers want to make the best programmes they can with the resources that they have, and often their teams are too small. The temptation to use free labour can be overpowering.

It's a Catch-22 situation – youngsters need work experience to boost their CVs, but they also need (and deserve) money to exist. All I can suggest is that if you are in this position you try to get everything that you can out of your work experience opportunity, in order to compensate for not being paid. Suck knowledge and contacts out of the people around you. And make yourself indispensable as soon as you can. If that happens, the company will soon start paying to avoid losing you!

In this chapter there are guides to the world of running, edit assisting and production coordination – the most likely work experience roles. You'll find dozens of tips on how to do them well. There are also some top tips on 'blagging': that is, getting stuff for nothing (or failing that, next to nothing). Blagging tips will come in useful if you're a runner, production coordinator, researcher (or just an ordinary human being who doesn't like paying full whack for everything!).

How to be an impressive runner

A PERSONAL VIEW

If you're a runner, you're basically a 'dogsbody'. What exactly you will be asked to do depends on the kind of programme on which you're working. If it's a cookery show, you may be asked to pop out and source ingredients. If it's a drama, you could be making notes and logging takes. If it's a studio game show, you might be herding contestants around the building. Whatever it is, you'll be making tea. Lots of it.

TV is more laid-back now than when I first started. In the 'good old days', a mixture of restrictive practices and megalomaniac directors could make shoots very scary places indeed. One director shouted at me for bringing a clipboard on set (I think he was 'clipboardophobic'), and a 'jobsworth' props guy threatened to send me to Coventry (that is, get me ignored by every union member) for giving a souvenir T-shirt to an audience member at the end of a show. That was his job you see, and in those days there was strict demarcation about who did what.

Things are generally less formal these days. You no longer get ceremonially shot for going through a gallery red light, or forgetting to ask permission from a floor manager to enter the studio, but it still isn't a good idea to ignore these traditional protocols. They exist for good reason. Walking through a red light distracts a busy director. The floor manager needs to know who is on set for health and safety reasons. You will impress people and gain brownie points if you adhere to the old rules. The best tip is: if you're unsure about something, ask the right questions to the right people at the right time – no easy matter in itself. Alternatively, just watch what everyone else is doing!

TV RUNNING: 15 TOP TIPS

1. **Don't be late**
   Tardiness shows a lack of commitment. If your transport arrangements are unpredictable, plan to arrive an hour early. People will be impressed by your diligence – and you may get the chance to do extra jobs during set-up – further enhancing your reputation and skill set.

2. **Volunteer for tasks**
   Don't wait to be asked to do something – volunteer yourself. The words I like to hear most from a runner when I'm up to my eyeballs directing a sequence is 'What can I do to help?' It shows a proactive nature, empathy and confidence – all good things.

3. **Be politely pushy**
   If you don't put yourself forward, you may end up standing around twiddling your thumbs. Remember, it's down to you to learn as much as you can, as quickly as you can. You need to create a good impression in your limited work experience time.

4. **Don't forget where you are in the TV 'food chain'**
   You may have a double first from Cambridge, but if the director tells you to jump, you say: 'How high?' It's also not a good idea to advise him on how to compose his shots on your first day!

5. **Detail is important**
   If you get the little things right, you might be given more responsibility. Do every job to the best of your abilities, be it tape labelling or lunch collecting. Even if the crew seem to be running around like headless chickens, somebody somewhere will notice if you are sloppy.

6. **Look out for people who may help you in the future**
   Making a busy person a cup of tea at the right moment can go down very well. The director for example. Directing a big shoot can be very stressful. A well-timed cup of tea from a smiling runner will be noted.

7. **You're called a runner, not a walker!**
   Imagine you're the director in this situation – the light's fading, the contributor's getting nervous and the presenter's irritated that you haven't wrapped yet. You need a new tape and the runner saunters back to the crew vehicle to fetch one as if they haven't a care in the world. Would you give them a good reference? Would you hire them for a paid position? No. If the runner comes back sweaty and breathless because they've run the whole way, the director realises that they're committed to the cause.

8. **Don't wander off**
   Stay close to whoever looks like they need help most, and get stuck in when you can.

9. **If you're not sure – ask, however 'stupid' the question may be**
   Being inquisitive is good, but be sensible – ask someone your 'stupid' question when they have time to answer.

10. **Be silent during takes and stand in the right place**
    Make sure that you're quiet, your mobile is switched off and you're standing behind the camera during filming. Also, don't look the actor or presenter in the eye – some don't like it.

11. **Be prepared for a long day**
    It's best not to have social plans on the evening of a shoot – things have a habit of running over.

12. **Dress appropriately**
    One runner I know turned up on a freezing December day in a T-shirt: no hat, no coat, no gloves – no common sense! He rapidly turned blue. He looked like a smurf by the end of the day – without the white hat that might have kept him warm.

13. **Be friendly to everyone and try to get more contacts**
    Email addresses and phone numbers are gold dust in TV. Keep networking!

14. **Get some business cards printed**
    You can get free samples on the internet. Order some business cards with your name, mobile phone number, email address and the word 'Runner' at the bottom. Hand these out to all and sundry – you never know who'll be hiring next. Also, leave some lying around in the production office, in the canteen and in the loos. Well, maybe not the loos…

15. **Enjoy yourself!**
    TV is great fun and it's full of characters. Do your utmost to enjoy every minute. However, that doesn't apply to another possible work experience position – the post-production runner role…

A PERSONAL VIEW

Nowadays, a post-production runner often fulfils the same role as an edit assistant. It's the only role in this book that I haven't done myself – officially. I have helped out in edit suites though, and supervised many edit assistants in my time, and they fall into two categories: great or hopeless.

This may be because getting work experience as an edit assistant is relatively easy. I say 'relatively', because getting any work in TV is hard. However, the edit assistant role is so tough, lonely and unglamorous that it leads to rapid turnover; consequently, more opportunities arise. Perhaps this manifests itself in less quality control and some, shall we say, less 'diligent' individuals managing to get in.

Let me tell you the story of a hopeless edit assistant and the effect his hopelessness had on an entire channel:

I was working on a series for Five. It was fast turnaround. We had to film the programme during the week, edit it straight away, then transmit the following Sunday. We had a base in Norwich, we were filming all around the country and the edit was at a post-production facility in London.

At the post-production facility you could never find the edit assistant when you needed him. When you did track him down and ask him to do something, he would tut and roll his eyes. He was more interested in sipping his skinny latte than arranging a tape transfer for you. But that's nothing – he was to make a mistake that would have serious ramifications…

I needed to check the edited shows in Norwich on DVD before they were transmitted because the programmes were a legal minefield. All the edit assistant in London had to do was post a DVD of the edited programme to me on the Thursday so I could watch it in Norwich on Friday, then any necessary changes could be made before it went out on Sunday. He forgot. I didn't get to see the programme in time, and it went out with a bad 'legal'. This necessitated us making a full on-screen apology before the next show was transmitted the following Sunday. One edit assistant's little mistake led to big repercussions for the whole channel.

However, if you do a brilliant job as an edit assistant you normally make rapid progress to other better paid positions, sometimes even the hallowed role of editor. Here is the inside track on the mysterious world of the edit assistant – and how to be good at it.

EDIT ASSISTING/POST-PRODUCTION RUNNING

Some elements of the job
- Making sure rushes (programme material) are logged and digitised into the system.
- Checking that all the relevant media is in when the editor arrives.
- Ensuring that tapes are in the right place at the right time.
- Organising lunches and snacks.
- Making lots of cups of tea and coffee!

What you need to know
- There are different types of edit systems, eg Avid and Final Cut Pro.
- There are different kinds of tapes, eg Digibeta, high definition (HD) and digital video camera (DVCAM).
- Tapes are slowly becoming obsolete – soon we will live in a tapeless world.
- Memory cards and hard drives are slowly taking over.

What you need to be able to do
Rushes management:
- Rushes need to be labelled properly and entered into the system.
- Don't drop a tape or eject one in the middle – it stretches the tape.
- 'Record inhibit' is important – if you come across a rushes tape that hasn't got the little red 'record inhibit' tab pressed, you should report it. This mistake leads to rushes being wiped over and lost forever.

Logging:
- Identifying the shots and content on each tape with timecodes, for example: '10.00.30 to 10.05.30 CU IV Bob, 10.05.30 to 10.07.20 BCU scars'.
- Use standard abbreviations and keep it simple – here's a good template: framing/content of shot/what the shot does.
- For framing, use acronyms: BCU (big close-up), CU (close up) WS (wide shot).
- For content, ditto: PTC (piece to camera) IV (interview) GV (general view). NG (no good). Just include important detail – eg IV and name.
- For what the shot does, use the correct terms – eg Pan L to R. Zoom in. Pull focus.

Digitising:
- This is importing what is on the tape into the edit system.
- Digitising is time-consuming and things can go wrong. For example, you can digitise two minutes rather than 20 minutes, you can import the footage at the wrong resolution, or you can mistakenly digitise the wrong tapes.
- You also need to try and avoid 'overfilling a partition' by importing too much media (pictures and sound) into the hard drive.
- Often, digitising is done overnight to maximise edit efficiency.
- You may be all on your own, so don't go stir crazy!

EDIT ASSISTING: SEVEN TOP TIPS

1. **Don't leave the room when you're digitising**
   That is when things go wrong. It may be boring and lonely, and extremely tempting to go down the pub for a swift half – but don't do it!

2. **Be honest**
   Often, digitisers are paid by the hour. If you're booked for 10 hours, the company will expect that amount of material to go in – it will be spotted if you try claiming for hours that you haven't worked.

3. **Be cheerful and helpful when assisting in the edit suite**
   Editing can be stressful for editors and directors. They can suffer from 'pre-viewing tension' and 'ludicrous schedulitis'. Anything you can do to cheer them up is always appreciated.

4. **Seize any chance to edit**
   I knew a runner at Anglia TV who was asked to cut 'selects' because an editor was ill. 'Selects' are sections of the programme to be sent off to the broadcaster to be edited into promotions. Luckily the runner had already acquired some basic edit skills by getting quick lessons here and there. She did a good job on the selects and got the next trainee editor job going.

5. **Apply Direct TV Training's 'golden rule'**
   Put yourself in the shoes of the stressed out editor or producer/director working late. How can you help them? Perhaps organise some food for them? Regular refreshments? Don't go home until you're certain that they don't need you anymore. It will be noted if you leave them hungry or thirsty!

6. **Do some extracurricular activities**
   It's a good idea to familiarise yourself with Photoshop and After Effects (Adobe programs) in your spare time. These are becoming increasingly useful for editors when dealing with stills and graphic sequences. An editor may ask you to work on some shots – great for the CV!

7. **Network**
   Make the most of any chance you get to talk to editors and producer/directors. Pick their brains about possible job openings and ask for tips on how to make progress. You may even progress to a more demanding work experience role – production coordinator.

A PERSONAL VIEW

Being a production coordinator is not my idea of fun. I went into TV to be out and about meeting people, going places and filming stories. Production coordinators don't get much of that. They are the unsung heroes (but more often heroines) of the TV world. Getting everyone organised, arranging locations, booking taxis and writing call sheets. Without them, it would all fall apart.

It's a really important job and detail is paramount. To prove the point, let me tell you about a near-death experience I had. In 2001 I fell 30 feet off the volcano Krakatoa and I was very lucky not to be seriously injured. If I had needed medical treatment I wouldn't have been able to get it. The phone number of Medevac (our emergency assistance service) on the call sheet was wrong.

That's just one extreme example of the importance of precision when you're a production coordinator. Something as simple as a typo error on a postcode for a location can send a crew to the wrong side of a city and lose valuable filming time. Not arranging parking for the crew? That results in a grumpy crew and, again, wasted time – and time is money.

It's a lot of pressure but the production coordinator role, and after that production management, really suits some people. They enjoy getting everything organised and sending the 'kids' off to Bolivia or Bognor, Sri Lanka or Skegness to film their pretty pictures. It's not for me – I like to be on the road. But whatever your role in TV, you need to have an understanding of what production coordinators do, because it is the most important job in TV.

HOW TO BE A GOOD PRODUCTION COORDINATOR: 13 TOP TIPS

1. **Be organised**
   A tidy desk is a tidy mind is a tidy shoot. You don't want to be scrambling around trying to find the number of the anti-venom supplier when the crew calls you from India to say they've run out and they're about to catch a king cobra!

2. **Be precise**
   Remember, phone numbers and directions have to be right. Double-check everything.

3. **Keep a 'to do' list of what needs to be done – and get ticking!**
   There is no better feeling than ticking things off a list. Keeping tabs on what you have and haven't done can prevent you from forgetting something really important because you don't like doing it.

4. **Keep a note of things that other people are supposed to be doing**
   As production coordinator you need to ensure that others are doing their jobs too. Researchers have to feed you information for the call sheet, production managers must keep you updated on the budget, etc. If they fall behind, it's you who will suffer.

5. **Make sure you have fall-back plans**
   When things go wrong, stay calm and action one of your fall-back plans. For example, one of my colleagues had a nightmare on a wildlife shoot in Cuba. The high definition camera was dropped in a river on the first day of filming. The production coordinator took too long to arrange a replacement. By the time the new camera arrived, the filming permit had run out and the whole shoot went down the drain.

6. **Always be available**
   Tea breaks? Lunch breaks? Sleep? These are luxuries you may have to do without. A cameraman friend of mine was run over while filming in Australia. The second person the programme producer called (after the ambulance) was the production coordinator, to sort out the medical insurance, a flight home for the casualty and a new cameraman. It was the middle of the night, but she'd arranged the lot by breakfast – and called the cameraman's wife to reassure her that everything was going to be fine. Impressive.

7. **Try to head off potential problems before they happen**
   It's better to fight a fire before it becomes a raging inferno (in fact, it's better to fight it before it even starts). Spotting oncoming problems and solving them in advance gets easier with experience. Put it this way: you only forget to book a taxi home for the presenter once!

8. **Help others whenever possible**
   TV is a team game: There's no 'I' in television (well, just a couple). If you help a colleague who is rushed off their feet, they are likely to repay the favour in the future. Even if they don't, you'll feel warm inside.

9. **Keep your producer/director aware of things that you have and haven't done**
   From a producer/director's point of view, I can assure you that it's nice to be kept informed. Some producer/directors like daily email updates; others prefer a verbal report every couple of days – but none like to be in an information vacuum. Early on in a production it's a good idea to find out how your boss likes to be kept in the loop, then work to that system – until they change their mind!

10. **If something goes wrong report it – don't try to hide it**
    As Richard Nixon (a US president impeached many years before you were born) would testify, 'It's not the mistake, it's the cover up that does for you.' Most producer/directors will forgive the occasional 'cock up' – as long as you do not repeat the same one regularly. However, none will be happy about someone trying to pull the wool over their eyes about a mistake. They are normally experienced enough to fix most problems with ease, if they find out about them early enough.

11. **The beauty of the cc**
Keep all relevant people in the loop by copying (ccing) them into your emails. It's only an extra keystroke, and extremely useful. If you accidentally cc someone who doesn't really need to know, they shouldn't find it too burdensome to press delete.

12. **Keep a good contacts book**
If you find a great contact, be it a tax adviser, taxi driver or taxidermist, note their details. You'll be using them again.

13. **Write excellent call sheets**
Production coordinators are in charge of the call sheet for the programme. Call sheets are so crucial that they warrant an entire section of their own...

The call sheet: the TV production bible

The call sheet is the document that goes to the whole crew, detailing what they need to know about the shoot. It is the most important thing in the production coordinator's world.

CALL SHEET ESSENTIALS: WHO, WHAT, WHEN, WHERE AND HOW

- **Who** needs to be there and all their contact details.
- **What** is the crew going to film? This will help the cameraman know what kit he needs. Will there be emotional interviews? That will help remind the sound recordist to bring his hankies and not to wear his flowery shirt.
- **When** do people need to be there? When will they wrap (finish)? When do they need to set off from the hotel? Is it a 10-minute journey or two hours? When is lunch?!
- **Where** do people need to be – the team needs location details and directions. Will the filming be interior or exterior? This will help the crew know what to wear. Where is the hotel at the end of the day? And note where the local hospital is, should there be an accident, etc.
- **How** are the crew going to source the kit? How are they going to get parked? How is the runner going to be able to afford a skinny mocha latte for the talent? All these things could be crucial to the smooth and happy running of the shoot – and that's down to you!

WRITING CALL SHEETS: TWO STRATEGIES

1. **Learn this mantra**
The best way to get your head round all this is to repeat the mantra at the top of the following page to yourself as you are writing the call sheet (preferably in your own head, rather than out loud – it's best not to scare your colleagues).

If it's not on the call sheet, it won't happen!
If it's not on the call sheet, it won't happen!
If it's not on the call sheet, it won't happen!

2. **Another approach is to imagine you are each crew member reading it**
   You are the cameraman. Is everything you need to know in the call sheet? You are the director. Is everything you need to know included? You are the presenter. Is everything you need to know there?

   You get the idea. You don't need to dress up or impersonate their voices, just put yourself in their shoes. For example, you are the cameraman: can you see where you are going, when you need to be there and what you are filming? Now you're the sound recordist. Does it say what the location is like?

   This thought process can help you avoid making terrible mistakes. For example, you're the famous presenter and you get a call sheet that contains your personal contact details for everyone to see. How are you going to respond?

   a. Call your agent and insist that the coordinator's head is brought to your tent.
   b. Call the producer and insist that the coordinator's head is brought to your tent.
   c. Call the head of the channel and insist that the coordinator's head is brought to your tent.

   Answer: Probably all of the above!

On that note, write a line at the top of the call sheet reminding the crew not to leave it lying around on set. You don't want contributors reading the call sheet, especially if it contains sensitive information about the programme.

Now that you've mastered the craft of call sheets, it's time for you to learn another essential skill for production coordinators, runners, researchers and, indeed, anyone who loves a bargain.

'Blagging': the art of getting something for nothing

A PERSONAL VIEW

Blagging isn't to everyone's taste. My wife, for example: she stunned me and the salesman in a Turkish bazaar by actually paying more for a vase than the price on the label. However, in the television industry, blagging skills are essential. Normally you're doing it with a stranger over the phone; sometimes it's face-to-face. In this era of reduced budgets and tight schedules, good blagging means getting more 'bang for your buck'. Any self-respecting TV person will have a tale of their favourite blag. (Mine include three white doves free of charge on a Sunday morning, forty free cinema tickets and a weekend for two at Eurodisney.)

Blagging is great fun and can make all the difference to the production value of your programme. If you can get props on-screen that look like a million dollars but cost you nothing, you're saving money which can be spent on other areas (plus you can tell your mum you got the Golden Fleece the actor is wearing – free of charge!).

BLAGGING: 15 TOP TIPS

1. **As with anything in life, if you don't ask, you don't get**
   Be prepared to be a bit of a 'Del Boy' with companies (Del Boy was a character played by David Jason in the 1980s sitcom *Only Fools and Horses*. He is the god of blagging). As Del Boy would testify, a cheeky haggle isn't going to upset anybody. They may even find it endearing!

2. **Turn on the charm – and make them laugh**
   Flattery goes a long way. And try to use humour early. Make a joke about the presenter. Say that the star hates paying over the odds for her knickers and insists you do the same for the safety vests you're trying to get for the crew.

3. **Remember to use 'spin'**
   You could say that your programme is a 'channel flagship', and that it's going to be repeated many times. Perhaps you can convince them that the viewer demographic is housewives with disposable income – the same people who buy the company's products.

4. **Go local rather than calling a national chain**
   Local stores are more likely to lend things for nothing. National chains have to call head office, which costs you time and effort – you will need to send an email and chase it up.

5. **Ask colleagues for advice**
   Where do they normally get things from for their shows?

6. **Play on the fact that ordinary people want to be involved in TV**
   It's a bit of sparkly glamour in their lives, something they can tell their kids about when they get home: 'You'll never guess who I got a call from at work today. Mr Tumble's best mate from the BBC. He was after some custard pies. Free of charge because Mr T is skint. I gave him a dozen.'

7. **Appeal to their business instincts**
   Tell them that millions/thousands/dozens of people will see their product and it won't cost them a penny. To officially advertise their product on TV would cost them thousands of

pounds, but you will do it for nothing because you like the sound of their voice. (See, it begins to get blurred: who's selling and who's buying.)

8. **Once you've got a deal, see what else you can blag**
   If a hotel wants to charge you £30 per person per night, ask if they can throw in breakfast and a packed lunch for free. Mention that, although you can't guarantee it will make the final edit, you'll ask the director to get a shot of the star walking into their fine establishment. 'Photos of the staff with the presenter? No problem!'

9. **Be confident with people**
   You're in TV. The best job in the world. You know stars. In fact, you're going to be a star yourself some day. They're lucky you've gone to the trouble to pick up the phone and dial their number!

10. **Never accept their first price**
    People can always afford to do things cheaper. A shop will not lose money by offering something for less – they'll just make a smaller profit. If a company wants £50 for a product, they'll probably take £45. If you can save £5 twenty times during pre-production, you will come in £100 under budget. More money for the end of series party!

11. **Try to talk to the boss when haggling**
    The boss can make the decision there and then without having to get clearance from anyone else. Remember, time is precious.

12. **Offer something in return**
    Make them an offer they can't refuse: a DVD of the show, a signed photo of the star, your undying gratitude for the rest of eternity? In an emergency you can offer a 'with thanks' credit, but make sure that you check with the producer first – there are strict guidelines about 'with thanks' credits. Giving them a plug on your company website is usually fine but again, be sure to check with your producer before offering it.

13. **Add good 'blagees' to your contacts book**
    Remember, your contacts book isn't just about getting you another job. It should be full of people that can help you (or others) in a wide variety of ways. Producers love it when they ask a production coordinator to source a purple unicorn and the coordinator says, 'No problem, in my contacts book I've got someone who can get you two – and throw in a pink dodo for free.'

14. **Stay one step ahead when closing the deal**
    Get them to quote prices including VAT – in that way, you are already saving money. If they say, 'We can do things for cash', it means they are not putting it through their books and should be able to do you an even cheaper deal.

15. You can always go back

If you have tried elsewhere unsuccessfully and it turns out that the first place you tried is actually the best option, you can still go back to them and pay their original price.

If all those tactics fail, try these emergency TV protocols, in the following order:

1. 'If I don't get this for free my boss will fire me.'
2. Burst into tears – 'I've been working through the night trying to get this sorted.'
3. Offer to go out on a date with them, but only if they buy all the drinks (after all, what kind of blagger would you be otherwise?).

So you've read all about your potential early roles in TV and absorbed some fantastic tips on how to be brilliant at them. Now we move onto the next jobs on the TV career ladder. You are about to find out how to do them so well that you're never short of work!

Chapter 5:
TV Research:
Essential Skills And
Tricks Of The Trade

Chapter 5: TV Research: Essential Skills And Tricks Of The Trade

I started as a researcher in the Science Department at YTV in 1988. It seems a lifetime ago, and in many ways it is. The industry has changed enormously since then. There was only one computer in the whole department when I joined. There were no mobile phones to get you out of trouble, there was no internet to do basic research and you couldn't communicate with colleagues via email. We had several months to make each show and money hardly seemed to be an issue at all. Contracts were nice and long. In fact, television was perceived as a job for life, with pension rights, sickness benefits and even a Christmas bonus! Yes, it was a different world.

However, some things have stayed the same. A good researcher is still worth their weight in gold. And being a researcher is still the best job in TV. Why? Because you are doing something challenging and creative. You are usually part of a fun-loving team that likes to work hard and play hard. You get to go on shoots in interesting places where you meet fascinating people. And you don't have all the pressure of actually delivering the programme – like us poor old producers.

That is not to say that the job is stress free. It isn't – and being a researcher does age you fast. However, it's the best job in the best industry in the world. So that's pretty good going.

This chapter contains numerous tips on how to be a great TV researcher. It isn't possible to include everything – that would require a book 10 times as big – but it covers most of the important stuff.

Research skills: an introduction

The four main categories of TV research are: **stories, people, locations** and **facts**.

1. FINDING *STORIES* AND HELPING FILM THEM

TV is all about telling stories. Part of a researcher's role is to find stories and help them come to life on screen.

2. FINDING AND INTERVIEWING *PEOPLE*

You need people to help tell the stories. As a researcher you need to track down good people and persuade them to take part in the programme. Then you suggest the best potential contributors to the producer/director, keep the ones the producer/director chooses on board and then possibly interview them on camera.

3. FINDING AND SETTING UP *LOCATIONS* FOR FILMING

You must be able to source good locations for filming and secure affordable access to them.

4. *FACT-CHECKING*

This is the only bit of TV research which has anything in common with academic research. Occasionally you may be asked to fact-check a commentary script, in order to make sure that the writer isn't being too economical with the truth. Some channels (for example National Geographic) expect every fact in a script to be double-sourced: ie established to be true from two reputable sources.

Research skills: the five resources

The five resources that researchers use are: ***phone***, ***internet***, ***email***, ***people*** and ***post***.

1. PHONE

Phone bashing' is a dying art, but it is the most important research skill of all. You need a good phone manner to be a researcher. How can you check that a potential contributor can string a sentence together without it? How can you blag a good deal out of a location owner? How can you reassure a nervous contributor that they won't regret coming on your programme and revealing all?

2. INTERNET

The internet is a tremendous resource for stories, facts, locations and people – as a first stage. However, don't rely on it: there's a lot of rubbish on the internet too. You must double-check each fact (on reputable sites) and use the phone to sound out potential people, stories and locations.

3. EMAIL

Email is obviously great for a number of reasons, but it has its problems. It's easy to send an email and assume that someone has read it, but the problem is, some people rarely check their emails. If it's important, follow up with a phone call. Emails are useful for covering your back: you can use them as proof that you have (or have not) done something. However, it's very hard to gauge tone from an email: what might be intended as an amusing joke when written can seem like an offensive jibe when read. A straightforward request when written can come across as a rude order when read. It's wise to be aware of this.

4. PEOPLE

Most TV research is about talking to people. At the end of the day they are going to be talking on your programme, so they need to be able to talk to you. The best training I ever had for being a TV researcher was working behind a bar when I was a student. I learnt how to have a conversation with anyone, from drunks about to be chucked out to upper class toffs coming in for their annual Christmas sherry. A researcher needs to be a good talker, a good listener and a good reader of people. Most importantly, they need to have a genuine interest in what makes people tick. That is what being a TV researcher is all about.

5. POST

People often hear what they want to hear over the phone, so post is the best way to confirm important things such as shoot details and transmission information. It also can be a good way to trace people when all you have is their address. However, post is slow and TV hates slow. If you're in a rush, it's better to call a local taxi company and get them to hand-deliver a letter that you've faxed to them for £10. Or, if you need to talk to someone urgently, get a taxi driver to go round with a mobile phone and hand it over when the person opens the door. Quick quick quick – that's the way The World Of TV likes it.

ROOKIE RESEARCHERS: 15 TOP TIPS TO GET YOU STARTED

1. **Get a calendar**
    Put up a printed-out calendar of the pre-production and production period where you can see it. It helps to focus your attention as the shoot looms.

2. **Print out a contacts list**
    Keep a printed copy of all your production teams' phone numbers handy. A contacts list in your back pocket often comes to your rescue. What if your computer goes down? Or you urgently need to call someone but you're down the pub?

3. **Keep back-ups of important information**
    Losing your precious contact information and not having it backed up anywhere else is a total nightmare. My contacts book was stolen a couple of years ago from the boot of my car, along with my laptop and my memory stick back-up. I lost hundreds of contact details, including those of Vinnie Jones and the Nobel Prize winner Professor Fred Hoyle. Two ends of the evolutionary spectrum gone in one fell swoop.

4. **Read shooting scripts**
Your producer will almost certainly generate a shooting script before going out to film. Ask if you can read it: this will give you advance warning on what you will be asked to do on location (plus it looks like you're really interested in the final show – which creates a good impression).

5. **Preparation is key**
Prepare for filming fastidiously and distribute all the relevant information to all the relevant people. No one likes being left out.

6. **Remember your position on the TV 'food chain'**
You're not experienced enough to tell the rest of the team that they're doing it all wrong … yet!

7. **Don't procrastinate**
Do what you have been asked to do as quickly as possible. Create a 'To Do' list and get ticking.

8. **Communicate effectively with your producer**
Remember the Golden Rule: put yourself in someone else's position. If you were the producer, you would want to hear both the good news and the bad news as quickly as possible. There is nothing worse than feeling in the dark, so keep your producer well briefed and up-to-date.

9. **'Bring me solutions, not problems!'**
If you do have bad news, go to your producer with a solution (or two) already in mind.

10. **Organise release forms**
Please be on top of the 'boring' stuff like this. Your hardworking producer/director doesn't want to be bothered by it. Take the contributor, location and photo release forms to the shoot and get them signed as soon as you arrive. These forms are essential. Don't wait until the end of the day to get them signed – you may need to rush to the next location, or the contributor may have become emotional during the interview and it feels inappropriate to ask. Get them signed ASAP!

11. **Use your initiative**
For example, if you are sent on a recce to check out the location and contributors in advance of the shoot, take a digital camera so that you can take photos. This will impress – especially if you do it without being asked. Even better, take a camcorder and film the location and contributors. You'll get valuable filming practise, your producer will note that you can shoot, and the contributor will begin to get used to being filmed. All good.

12. Assess potential contributors

Part of your role is filtering which contributors to suggest to your producer for inclusion in the programme. If in doubt, drop them and find someone else. You will look foolish if a useless contributor turns up for a shoot because you have deluded yourself that they would be fine. And always have back-ups on standby in case someone drops out at the last minute.

13. Volunteer for tasks during filming

The more you create a good impression by putting yourself forward for tasks, the more responsibility you'll be given – and the faster you'll move up the career ladder.

14. After filming, send out 'thank you' letters to all and sundry

It's important to keep your contributors sweet at all times. And your experts. And your on-screen talent. And the people who gave you locations. You never know when you'll need them again.

15. Behave yourself at the end of series party!

Don't throw up on the dancefloor. If you do feel obliged to, at least do it entertainingly. If you incorporate it into a dance routine, you might get away with it!

As you have just seen, there is a lot to being a TV researcher. But that's just for starters. Now, on to some more advanced stuff…

Advanced research skills: people and story finding

A PERSONAL VIEW

Finding stories, and contributors to tell those stories, is an essential skill for a TV researcher – and it's one that can easily go wrong.

One of my first tasks in TV was to find an HIV-positive prostitute for a 1980s ITV show called *Where There's Life*, presented by Miriam Stoppard. I was sent to Leith, an area of Edinburgh, which was the 'AIDS capital' of Europe at that time.

With the help of the vice squad I tracked down Audrey, one of the most notorious prostitutes in town. After 'charming her' I drove Audrey and her boyfriend/pimp to Leeds for the studio. It was recorded 'as live'. The show didn't get off to a good start. Miriam went up to Audrey and said, 'So Audrey, you're a prostitute?' and Audrey replied, 'No, I'm not!'

Miriam immediately shouted 'Julian!' at the top of her voice. I scuttled across and said, 'But Audrey, you are a prostitute.' She replied, 'I know – but if I say that, I'll be arrested.'

'Good point. How about we put a wig on your head and call you Deirdre?' 'All right,' she said, and went off to get wigged up. When Miriam finally interviewed her, she claimed that she made all her punters wear condoms, even for 'manual relief'. Not very believable…

To make things worse, all the HIV-positive drug users I had booked for the audience were falling asleep behind Audrey/Deirdre, because they had been injecting in the YTV toilets. After the show, one of them broke a glass and bled all over a table in the YTV bar, leading to a major security alert. The next day they all went on a shoplifting spree around Leeds because the local store detectives didn't recognise them, unlike back home in Edinburgh. The situation got so bad that the police called YTV and told us to get them out of town immediately. I took Audrey to the train station personally, gave her £25 and a kiss (on the cheek), put her on the train, breathed a huge sigh of relief and went back to my flat.

Half an hour later I was paying my elderly landlady the rent downstairs. My girlfriend suddenly burst in and shouted 'Julian, it's your prostitute on the phone. She says she won't leave town until you give her more money.' My landlady almost had a heart attack. She evicted me soon after.

In that programme the story was already in place when I came on board. It was investigating HIV transmission in young people. When I joined the show as a researcher, I was given a clear remit about the type of people that I needed to find. That is often the case. A development team will come up with the idea for a programme, get it commissioned (if they're very lucky), then researchers are brought on board to find stories to fit into the programme. These stories tend to come from people, so it's fair to say that people finding is the most important part of a researcher's job. Here are some people-finding strategies.

PEOPLE FINDING: EIGHT STRATEGIES

1. **Put out a 'trail'**
   In other words, during or after a programme, transmit an appeal for contributors to take part in an upcoming show with a phone number so they can get in touch. This is a good way of targeting a large amount of people. Shows such as The Jeremy Kyle Show and Trisha Goddard use this approach a lot. The calls that come in are chased up by the production team. However, a lot of 'odd' people tend to call in, so this can be quite time-consuming.

2. **Advertise in magazines and papers**
   Placing an advert in a newspaper or magazine is a good way to get your message out to lots of potential contributors. However, you need to place your advert in the best magazine or newspaper in order to attract the attention of the kind of people you want on the show. Plus adverts cost money – and money is usually tight.

3. **Look for stories in magazines and papers**

Magazines and papers are a good way of finding people with personal stories. Magazines such as *Bella*, *Now* and *Chat* have lots of personal interest stories. Once you've found a story of interest, you can try to trace the contributors via BT Directory Enquiries, the electoral register (on the internet) or by contacting the magazine journalist directly. However, most journalists will be too busy to dig out contacts. They will want you to pay for their phone numbers, or at least give them a story in exchange. It's better (and more fun) to do your own detective work.

4. **Radio appeals**

Different types of people listen to different types of radio stations, so you must make sure that you get your message out on the right stations at the right times. When contacting radio stations, ask to be put through to the newsdesk. Think of an angle, and offer your producer or presenter for an interview, assuming that they are happy to give up their time. Breakfast shows have the biggest audiences, so aim for those. If you end up in the Alan Partridge 4am slot you might not get many responses – unless you're looking for taxi drivers.

5. **Local news agencies**

These are good to contact when looking for people in a specific area with a compelling story to tell. However, you will be charged for the contributor's contact details. Be careful that you don't get conned: make sure that the contributors you are paying for really want to be on TV and are good value.

6. **Posters and flyers**

These can work if you have the resources and time to put up posters and hand out flyers, but it's crucial that you target the right places. It also takes confidence to hand out flyers to strangers (having said that, if you haven't got confidence, you shouldn't be in TV!). Handing out flyers can work if you're looking for, say, attractive, outgoing single people for a late-night series and you hand out flyers in pubs on a Friday night. However, this method is not so good when looking for people with emotionally engaging personal stories!

7. **The internet**

There are hundreds of sites on the internet where you can post messages advertising for people who want to be on TV. Perhaps the best known is Beonscreen.com (www.beonscreen.com). However, when searching on the net you need to focus your efforts. Are you looking for swingers to talk about open marriages? Or model plane enthusiasts to talk about their hobby? Perhaps you need someone with chronic halitosis to try out a new mouthwash? Different people inhabit different regions of the internet (unless they're a swinging model plane enthusiast with halitosis).

8. **'Cold calling'**

This is used only as a last resort, as it is hit-and-miss and rarely works. Most researchers have a story about booking someone for a talk show by calling a pub the night before the studio and asking the landlady to do a 'shout out' – but these are often fictitious! Quite often you will waste time calling dozens of pubs, hairdressers and gyms and get nowhere.

ANOTHER PERSONAL VIEW

One of the most common questions that people in TV are asked is: 'Where do you get those people?' The answer is, everywhere and nowhere. There are many different ways of finding contributors for your programmes – and no golden solution to every people-finding challenge.

The most important tip is to be persistent, and not to go for the first person you find. Your show relies on you finding the best, not the easiest. The more people you speak to, the more choices you'll have to offer to the producer. And more choice means a better final product. Think of your producer as a chef and you as his ingredient supplier: the more options you give him to cook with, the nicer the final meal will be. More choice also means that you'll have fall-back options, if and when you get dropouts.

I was once asked to find a 'token sucker' in New York to appear on a First Tuesday documentary called *Subway City* about the New York underground. A token sucker is someone who sucks tokens out of the subway turnstiles and sells them. I was also looking for a subway comedian (someone who tells jokes on the trains for money). I was given a phone number of a subway comic by the person I sat next to on the flight over to America. She was being deported after serving five years for drug smuggling and had a few 'interesting' contacts in New York. I kept calling the number she gave me but every time I phoned, a very rude woman answered and refused to put me through to the guy in question. This went on for weeks, but I wasn't to be denied, and kept calling until finally he answered.

I couldn't believe it when he told me he wasn't the subway comedian after all. I don't know why, but out of sheer desperation I asked him if he knew any token suckers – and out of the blue he admitted he'd been doing it for years! We got on like a house on fire, I charmed him and he agreed to come on the programme. He was also a porn star in his spare time. When I asked him if he was worried about AIDS, he said that wasn't a problem for him – all his co-stars were on the pill! He wasn't the sharpest knife in the drawer but he was a great interviewee. The moral of that story is that if you try long enough and hard enough, you will find your man (or woman) – but they often crop up in the most unexpected places.

It is not only ordinary people with compelling stories that researchers need to find, they also may need to source experts and celebrities.

Expert finding

An expert can make or break your programme. If they are engaging, passionate and willing to talk in a way that captivates the viewer, the topic you've been stressing about for months can come to life. However, if they're dry and monotonous, fearful that their peers will feel they're 'dumbing down' by appearing on TV and unwilling to compromise on their standard 'stood at the front of a lecture theatre' style, you're stuffed. Some experts insist on using complicated jargon and three-letter acronyms (TLAs). This can leave viewers feeling confused and annoyed.

The best way to get a captivating expert for your programme is good phone research. Call someone who has already filmed the expert you're considering in the past. Did he perform when the camera started rolling, or did he become nervous and withdrawn? You can also check out videos featuring him on the internet. Is what he said scientifically respected? The best way to assess this is by talking to his peers and seeing how much work he's had published, and in which journals. Find out all this before you advocate him to your producer, and have a reserve expert up your sleeve just in case your producer doesn't rate the one you're advocating.

EXPERT FINDING: FIVE TOP TIPS

1. **Remember most experts have written books**
   So a good place to find experts is Amazon.com. This lists authors of books about specific areas and their publishers' details. To contact the expert, go through the publisher, whose contact details you'll be able to find through BT.com or Yellow Pages (Yell.com). Another handy site is www.findatvexpert.com.

2. **Academia can be bitchy**
   When checking whether your experts are respected in their field, beware of their peers being jealous and not being objective in what they say. They might have a vested interest, especially with research grants becoming increasingly elusive.

3. **Experts are often at universities**
   Obvious, I know – but I just thought I'd mention it. You can find experts through reading university directories and calling their departments. However they will usually request that you go through the university press office.

4. **Experts often belong to professional associations**
   You can often trace an expert through their professional association. My favourite is BAPS – the British Association of Plastic Surgeons. Great name, bearing in mind that they spend most of their time doing breast enlargements.

5. **Don't panic**
   As is the case with all TV, you will find that expert contributors drop out. Whatever happens, don't panic. You always end up with someone better.

A PERSONAL VIEW

I have had the good fortune to work with loads of celebrities: Lorraine Kelly, Ulrika Jonsson, Vinnie Jones, Gloria Hunniford, Judy Finnigan, Andrew Sachs, Miriam Stoppard, Carol Vorderman, Mark O'Shea, Dennis Waterman, Julie Christie, Eamonn Holmes, James Woods and Trisha Goddard to name but a few (well, actually, to name all of them). By and large, the more famous someone is, the nicer they are. Gloria bought me a lovely Christmas present; Trisha invited me to her 50th birthday party and Lorraine asked me and my son back to her Spanish villa for lunch after a voiceover record in Marbella.

That being said, Mark once threatened to 'smash my face in' on a US Airforce plane parked on the tarmac at Guam Airport; and Vinnie said he'd go 'effing mental' if he didn't get back to Sheffield from Alton Towers in half an hour – a timescale that would defy the laws of physics.

Hollywood icon Burt Reynolds actually refused to work with me on Stunt School. I'm hoping it was the subject matter that put him off, rather than a fear that he would be compelled to beat me up. A school for stuntmen? Perish the thought! It's never dull in the world of celebrity. Except when you're waiting for them to turn up.

1. THERE ARE VARYING LEVELS OF CELEBRITY – DEAL WITH THEM DIFFERENTLY

TV programmes are becoming increasingly celebrity-oriented and some celebrities have become known as 'national treasures': Joanna Lumley, Stephen Fry, Victoria Wood, etc. They aren't hard to find, but they are hard to book – most are busy until 2082. If you do persuade one to come on your programme, do not upset them. They are more important than God – and they definitely do exist.

2. WORK HARD TO CAST THE RIGHT CELEBRITY FOR YOUR SHOW

Don't forget there is another strata of celebrity: not so much 'national treasure', as 'national change in your pocket'. Former Big Brother contestants et al. Whatever your show, inevitably there will be a celebrity out there who would love to appear on it for the right fee. One of your jobs as a researcher may be finding available celebrities and presenting them to your producer to consider. Here are some places to look:

- Spotlight.com
- Theredpages.co.uk
- Celebritiesworldwide.com

3. BE CAREFUL WHEN CONTACTING AGENTS

Celebrity agents can be a nightmare, or they can be incredibly helpful – they are either one or the other. I'm convinced that most of the diva stories you hear about Hollywood stars being difficult are down to their agents making unrealistic demands to impress their clients:

'I'll get your winnebago flown to Paris, John, no problem.'
'She must have her hotel suite painted purple, or she isn't coming.'
'Don't let anyone look my client in the eye. How can she emote?'

How many of these are really down to the stars themselves? And how much of it is agents showing off, I wonder…

Anyway, here are some agency websites for your information:

- New Faces – www.newfacestalent.co.uk
- James Grant Media Management – www.jamesgrant.co.uk
- Noel Gay – www.noelgay.com
- Media Ambitions – www.mediaambitions.com
- Arlington Enterprises – www.arlingtonenterprises.co.uk
- Jeremy Hicks Associates – www.jeremyhicks.com

Please note: even if you have the personal contact details of a celebrity, it is still important that you go through their agent to make an initial contact about a programme. If you contact the celebrity direct, you are likely to annoy them and their agent. Especially the agent (and you don't want to annoy the agent – they can get you killed).

So you've found your people/expert/celebrity. Congratulations! However, there's more to being a TV researcher than just that.

Location finding and fact-checking

Location finding and background fact-checking are also part of a researcher's remit. Finding locations is very similar to finding people. If you combine the people finding skills discussed in this chapter with the blagging tips in Chapter 4 and the recce tips mentioned in Chapter 8, you will be in good shape.

As far as fact-checking is concerned, the internet is usually the place to go. But you must make sure that you go to reputable sites and double-source everything. Here are some good sites:

- Martindale's – The Reference Desk – www.martindalecenter.com
- Onelook (indexes more than 6m words) – www.onelook.com
- Concise Columbia Electronic Encyclopedia – www.encyclopedia.com
- Online phonebooks at Teldir on the Infobel site – www.infobel.com/teldir
- Maps (of pretty much everywhere) – www.multimaps.com

As you can see, there is a lot to the researcher's role. People, location and fact-finding can be really good fun. It's a bit like being a private investigator, but without the gun. However, that's only half of it; the most important part of the researcher's remit is yet to come…

Talking to contributors

A PERSONAL VIEW

Talking to contributors is one of the best parts of the job. If you are a good researcher, you genuinely like meeting people. It's one of the main reasons you do the job. However, much of the time you don't actually meet them, you talk to them over the phone, and that is full of jeopardy.

One of my first jobs was on a hospital documentary series called *Jimmy's*. It was big in the 1990s, regularly getting more than 10m viewers. I was trying to get hold of a patient before he came in for his operation. I phoned him at home, and a deep husky voice answered, 'No, he's not here. Try calling back later.' I replied 'Thank you very much. Are you his brother?' There was a pause, then the curt reply, 'No, I'm his wife'. For weeks I dreaded bumping into her along a dark hospital corridor.

Phone skills are important for researchers. Nowadays budgets are so small and schedules so tight that often there isn't time to go and see people face-to-face. You need to make judgements through a very unnatural process: a phone call with a stranger. You can't see their face or body language. It's much harder to establish rapport, to gauge how someone will perform on camera, to assess whether they'll actually turn up on the day – but it has to be done. So I've come up with lots of tips for you.

INTERVIEWING CONTRIBUTORS OVER THE PHONE: 20 TOP TIPS

1. **Be chatty and friendly**

   You need a good phone manner – it's important to be open, confident and friendly.

2. **Ignore the people around you**

   It may seem strange, having intimate conversations with strangers over the phone in an office full of people whom, you're convinced, are straining to hear every word – but you soon get used to it. The funniest thing I overheard while working on Trisha was, 'So, were your orgasms better as a man or as a woman?'

3. **Be a chameleon**

   You need to talk differently on the phone to a drug addict compared to a public school teacher. If your contributor throws swear words liberally into most sentences, you should do the same, so they'll feel more at ease. Early in the conversation you should try to get a feel for how to deal with the contributor. If they have a sad story, you'll need to be gentle and sympathetic, a friendly ear to listen to them. If you're looking for people to take part in a dating show, you'll have to be lively and full of energy to see if they can be outgoing too.

4. **Name drop the presenter**

   If your show is presented by a household name, use that to your advantage. Your conversation could go as follows. '[Insert star's name] is really interested in your problem/story and can't wait to meet you.' (Okay – it's a lie, but you're a TV researcher, not a nun.)

5. **Be clear about what you want**

   Once you've established a (phone) relationship, let them know as soon as possible exactly what will be required of them. The number of times I've had a long conversation with a potential contributor and right at the end they've said, 'Oh, I don't want to appear on TV, I thought you were just calling to chat!' I should have been more upfront from square one.

6. **Sell your show!**

   Give them the hard sell, but remember, what you say will be influenced by the genre of programme. Saying how much fun it is going to be won't wash with a bereaved mum coming on to talk about losing her son in a car crash. Talking about how the programme's aims are to get people to drive more carefully, might. The 'fun' approach applies to game shows, not hard-hitting documentaries.

7. **Think of your strategy before you call**

   Your strategy for persuading a serial adulterer to come on the programme will be different to your approach when talking to the woman he betrayed. In fact, you might not be the right person to make the call to the woman at all. A male researcher should have a blokey chat with the adulterer, and a female researcher should have a sympathetic chat with the unhappy wife. Don't make the call if you're wrong for it.

8. **People will mirror your phone manner**
   If you're friendly and confident, people will respond to it. If you're downbeat, you'll bring their energy levels down and make them less likely to make the effort to appear on the show.

9. **The 'Five Number Protocol'**
   One of the oldest tips in TV is: never put the phone down until you've got another five phone numbers. The idea is to drain your contributor of all their contacts. This can be particularly fruitful with experts. Often you will find that a contact of the person you are talking to is actually a better option than them.

10. **Listen out for other stories**
    This can change your career. A few years ago I was working on a current affairs programme and phoned a plastic surgeon to enquire about cosmetic surgery on teenagers – a hot topic at the time. He happened to mention that he knew someone doing cosmetic surgery on children with Down's Syndrome. I spotted that this was a much better story. We ended up making a hit documentary about it and I got to fly to New York to pick up an award from the Discovery Channel. All expenses paid. Result.

11. **Be realistic about the contributor**
    Objectively assess over the phone what the contributor can bring to your show. Are they a good talker? Have they got a good story? Are they reliable, or is there a good chance that they'll let you down? It may be that you haven't booked a contributor for ages and you are beginning to sweat about whether your contract is going to be renewed, but don't let that cloud your judgement. If that fear leads to you booking in an inarticulate oaf for the show whose story isn't believable, you'll be stuffed anyway.

12. **Source checking**
    It's critically important that you source check your contributors and verify their stories. A hoaxer could end your career. And your producer's. And your presenter's. And they won't like that. Cross-reference their story with other people in it. Talk to their mother about it. (Mums never lie, do they?) Check that their name, phone number and address match the electoral register. If in doubt, don't use them. It just isn't worth it.

13. **Try to get as much information as possible without scaring the potential contributor off**
    People are wary of journalists, so don't fire questions at them like a journalist might. Get the information in a more conversational way.

14. **Don't call their situation their 'story'**
    Some people get edgy if you do that. It belittles what they're going through.

15. Don't let them realise that you're writing everything down

If you can't do shorthand, you'll have to ask occasional redundant questions so that you can quietly catch up while they're replying.

16. Make sure, before starting, that they're comfortable and free to talk

Begin every phone conversation with: 'Is now a good time to talk?'

17. If possible, do the interview when they're alone in a room

Try to avoid doing it when the person they're talking about is in the room with them.

18. Go through a checklist of questions with participants

As well as covering everything about the story, you should go through the following:

- Do you have a criminal record?
- Do you have any disabilities or health problems?
- Do you have any mental health problems?

The mental health question is very important. If they do have mental health problems, find out what they are and whether they might affect their performance on the show. Could appearing on TV drive them over the edge? If in any doubt, don't invite them on.

19. Ask about any medication they take, and find out what it does

If they are on medication you should enquire about the doses they need. Netdoctor (www.netdoctor.co.uk) is a good site for information. You should also go through these questions with the source checks (ie other family members) so you know that they are telling the truth about things like drugs and criminal records. In addition, you should ask gently if they have ever attempted suicide – and, if so, how they did it, why and when. Keep your producer up-to-date on any concerns.

20. If they are any good, add them to your contacts book

Hopefully you are on your way to securing a fantastic contributor. If so, add them to your contacts. You may be able to trade their story with a news agency or another researcher – assuming that the contributor is happy for you to do so. Also don't forget something else may happen in their lives that is worth covering, and they could be participants again. Keep in touch with them with an occasional phone call – you never know what might crop up.

So, that's it for interviewing contributors over the phone. For tips on interviewing contributors face-to-face on camera, see Chapter 9 on page 149. That's much easier … not!

Keeping contributors on board

So you've found and chatted to your contributors, but you're not there yet. Another crucial researcher job is preventing them from dropping out of your programme.

A PERSONAL VIEW

'Droppy' contributors are part and parcel of TV. How often it happens to you depends on what kind of programme you're making. It can be a busy politician who suddenly can't squeeze you into his hectic schedule, a scientist who is suddenly getting cold feet because of peer pressure, or a nervous member of the public suddenly wondering whether it's a good idea to bare her soul in front of the watching masses.

Notice that I used the word 'suddenly' three times there. People often drop out of your show with no forewarning – and it can totally land you in it. Apart from trying to talk them back on board (tips to follow), the most important thing is to have a fall-back option to take to your boss: either a reserve contributor, or a reworking of that section of the show so 'we don't need them after all' (note: your boss may not fall for this).

Don't forget the Golden Rule: put yourself in your boss's position. Your producer won't be impressed if you to go them with a problem ('They've dropped') and no solution ('and I don't have a reserve!')

EIGHT REASONS WHY PEOPLE DROP OUT OF TV PROGRAMMES – AND WHAT NOT TO SAY IF IT HAPPENS TO YOU

If you play the conversations along these lines, you'll be shot (and quite right too)!

1. **They say 'The programme's going to make things worse at home'**
    Don't say, 'I can't deny the fact that your partner, your family, your kids, your friends, your kids' friends – pretty much everyone in your world – are going to see you on TV and have an opinion. Quite probably negative. You'd be mad to take the risk. Don't come on. You will regret it for the rest of your life.'

2. **'The programme's going to be bad for my career'**
    'Quite likely. If your boss sees you confessing to deviant practices on prime-time TV, he's not going to be impressed.'

3. **'People will think badly of me'**
    'Undoubtedly. Neighbours and acquaintances will be jealous that you're suddenly a minor celebrity in your hometown and will probably call you big-headed.'

4. **'I'm worried the programme isn't all it seems'**
    'You're right to be worried. I'm a two-faced researcher whose job it is to manipulate you for the good of the programme. I've probably told you several porkies already and we're only just starting to get to know each other.'

5. **'I can't be bothered'**
    'That's understandable. You'll have to take a day off work, come all the way down to the

65

studio, wait around for ages and be rushed here there and everywhere. After all that effort you'll probably only be in the final edited programme for about two minutes. What's the point?'

6. 'I'm poorly'
'You poor thing. The last thing you want is to make it worse by taking a long journey and sitting in a cold studio. You stay at home and wrap up warm.'

7. 'My car's broken down and I can't get there'
'That's a blow. Don't you worry about us. Just get it fixed when you can.'

8. 'I'm too nervous'
'I'm not surprised. Appearing on a TV programme in front of millions of people is way outside your comfort zone. Most sane people would be crazy to contemplate it.'

The right things to say in these eight specific scenarios are at the end of this section, but first, let's look at how to avoid dropouts in general.

How to avoid dropouts: the two main strategies

STRATEGY 1: STOP THEM DROPPING OUT BEFORE THEY DO IT

Make appearing on your programme totally stress-free for the contributor
If you can afford it, arrange a car to take them to the location. This is preferable to asking them to pick up a train ticket from the station, catch a train, make several connections and do all the other things that might stress them out.

Reduce what they need to sort out at home
Arrange childcare for them. Book a taxi to get their gran to their hospital appointment. See off any excuses as to why they can't show up before they make them.

Offer them cash if you can
If they're in work, agree on a generous loss of earnings fee to compensate them for taking a day off. If they don't work, calculate some lucrative expenses arrangement, but clear this with your producer first, as your budget might not allow it. (Note: this approach isn't allowed for criminals. Crime doesn't pay. Allegedly.)

Introduce them to the boss
Ask the producer/director to phone them to say 'hello' in advance of filming. This can make the contributors feel more valued. Plus if they drop out, they're not only letting you down, they're also letting down Mr/Ms Important.

Talk about what fun it will be

Tell them that people always enjoy filming and how much the team is really looking forward to meeting them. Make them feel as though they're about to be treated like royalty, even if your budget is more B&B than five-star hotel.

STRATEGY 2: NIP DROP OUTS IN THE BUD – TRY TO SEE THE PROBLEMS OFF AS SOON AS THEY START TO WOBBLE

Sound upset

As soon as they tell you they want to drop out, sound sincerely upset. Not because you're being inconvenienced – that's not an issue at all. You're sad because you really believe that dropping out is something they'll regret. Forever. Once you've established that you care, you need to find out why they're dropping out. You must convey convincingly how you'd hate them to lose the opportunity to:

- Change their lives
- Enjoy a fun-filled, unique experience
- Solve a serious problem
- Aid their career
- Be 'discovered' and become a star
- 'Make a difference'

Which of these options you choose depends on their initial motive for wanting to appear on the programme.

First let's assume it's a 'solve your problems' type of show. Here are some possible drop out scenarios and immediate response tactics:

They say 'Everything's all right now'

Ask them if the problems that led them to want to be on the programme have suddenly been solved elsewhere. The answer is usually no. Remind them that they obviously felt the problem was big enough to make the decision to get it sorted. If they don't come on, that problem will only get worse.

The 'What if?' strategy

If a couple says that they fear that appearing on the programme could threaten their relationship, get them to imagine the prospect of it all going to pot anyway and always having that huge 'What if?' in their lives. 'What if we'd gone on that show, would things be different?' That question could plague them for the rest of their lives.

'We're in this with you'

You may need to make them feel they're indebted to you. You and the rest of the production team have worked extra hard to make things work for them. Tell them, 'We're all in this together. We want to help you get this sorted.'

Don't make them feel defensive
You must not say things such as 'But you agreed' or 'You called us in the first place!' That will put them on the defensive straight away. The last thing you want is an argument.

Mention the star
You should say that the presenter is really keen to help them and has already worked out how they would do it. Remember, many viewers feel that they know presenters personally. They're practically friends – they are in their front rooms most days, after all.

If it is a quiz show:

Keep their eyes on the prize
If it's a quiz show, remind them that they're giving up the chance of a fantastic prize. Imagine reflecting on that for the rest of their lives. If there's a surprise element in the show, such as an expensive holiday, you may want to mention it now. Better that the contributors fake surprise on the show than not be there at all.

For all shows:

Talk – don't write
In a dropout situation, never try to write any details down. Concentrate fully on the conversation. You have enough to think about already – and if they think you're writing, they may get suspicious.

Remember you are 'friends'
When a contributor is dropping out, you really have to put everything into reinforcing your 'friendship' with them. You should tell them that you've personally prepared some special things for them at the hotel.

Get a colleague into the mix
If someone's dropping out and you're getting nowhere, you may feel that you're just not connecting with them. It could be your gender or even your accent. In that situation, ask a colleague to talk to them. Your colleague could call and say they're your boss. They'll use the same strategies that you did, but with a fresh voice. By pretending to be your boss they may make the contributors feel especially important and therefore more susceptible to persuasion.

Remember, it's probably nerves
TV may be part of your everyday world, but for the general public, the prospect of appearing on TV is very nerve-wracking. When people try to drop out, no matter what the excuse, it's

best to presume that the real reason is nerves. Here are some approaches you can use when they first start to sound anxious:

- If it isn't live, remind them that if anything goes wrong, they can just do it again.
- Some people get really nervous about talking straight to camera. If this isn't required, make sure they know this.
- If they're worried about running out of things to say, tell them that this never happens. Point out that the main part of the show will last X minutes – there's a good chance you've been on the phone with them for longer than that already.
- Remind them that when they're on the show they'll just be chatting, like they're doing with you right now. It's easy.
- Reassure them that they won't be asked questions they don't know the answer to. They're on to talk about their lives, who knows their lives better than them? Try to use humour whenever you can. I often say, 'We're not going to ask you, the capital of Nicaragua – honest!'

Let's go through the right way to play those earlier scenarios. Remember, the ones where you'd be shot if you said the wrong things?

1. **'The programme's going to make things worse at home'**
Persuade them that if they think their relationship could be badly affected by appearing on television, then it must be in a weak state. When they come on we can sort that. They would regret not getting it fixed, possibly forever.

2. **'The programme's going to be bad for my career'**
You should say straight away that they're not going to be put in a situation that will make them look foolish. Tell them that there's a good chance they'll actually get increased respect from their co-workers because they've been brave enough to confront the problem.

3. **'People will think badly of me'**
First, find out who these people are. If it's an older family member, point out that they come from an older generation when people didn't talk about emotions. If they say 'Gran says you shouldn't wash your dirty linen in public', you should say that the phrase 'dirty linen' is all about the stain of shame. Ask them if they have anything at all of which to be ashamed. They'll say 'No', so say straight away, 'You have no dirty linen to be worried about then'.

4. **'I'm worried the programme isn't all it seems'**
People are becoming wary of TV programmes that misinterpret them or make them look silly. The tabloids like to feature complaints from contributors who feel exploited by reality programmes. Efforts should be taken at all times to rid the contributor of these anxieties. You should emphasise straight away that you're nothing

like those awful ambush, car-crash TV type programmes. You're there to help them, not surprise them.

5. **'I can't be bothered'**
This should raise alarm bells on two levels: (1) they're dropping out; and (2) they're going to be lacklustre contributors anyway. If you really need them, it's time to go for the carrot and stick approach. The best carrot is money at this point. The best stick is to hint there could be bad implications, perhaps legally, if they were to drop out at this late stage. It can be very effective if this is done at the same time as mentioning the huge financial costs of cancelling a shoot. Always mention figures in their tens of thousands.

6. **'I'm poorly'**
Subtly find out if they really are poorly or whether it is just an excuse. If they're genuinely poorly, judge how bad the illness is and whether it is something they could recover from in your timescale. If they're actually dropping because of a routine doctor's or hospital appointment, tell them that you can phone the appropriate people, explain what's going on and get it changed. The power of TV!

7. **'My car's broken down and I can't get there'**
A transport problem is often the most common, annoying and preventable reason for drop out. When people are travelling to the programme venue they are at their most anxious. If a problem happens en-route it can cause contributors to get angry and use it as an excuse not to turn up. The production company should manage every facet of their transport, from doorstep to filming.

Note: contributors should always be dissuaded from travelling to filming in their own car. If they do this they could turn back at any time and mobile phone dead spots could mean that you can't contact them to talk them back on board. If you can't afford a taxi to get them all the way to your location (and most budgets don't stretch that far), make sure that the contributors know which name the train tickets are under and that they have all relevant booking codes in writing. Also, you should ensure that they know where to pick up their tickets. Often people queue at the station ticket office when they should be at customer services. Keep in touch with them at every stage of their journey to make sure that they're fine.

8. **'I'm too nervous'**
See above. Lots of responses to that.

If all this fails and they still drop out, tell yourself they probably wouldn't have been very good anyway!

So you've found the contributor, and you've kept them on board. Now we're almost at the point of actually filming them!

A PERSONAL VIEW

Setting up a shoot is often the best bit for researchers. Filming is always stressful because there is lots to do in a limited amount of time and lots of things can go wrong. This can lead to the people around you becoming stressed and abrupt, which isn't pleasant. Plus you can get stressed too, but you're not allowed to be abrupt. Remember your position on the 'food chain'. You're just above plankton – that's the runners. Think of yourself more as a prawn. Compared to the actual filming, setting up a shoot is quite laid-back. You chat to people over the phone, sometimes face-to-face. You write briefing notes. You might check out a location or two. All very civilised. Don't get me wrong – it can still get manic, but it isn't as bone-crushingly tense as filming can be.

SETTING UP THE SHOOT: 12 TOP TIPS FOR RESEARCHERS

1. **Keep an eye on the schedule**
   Normally the schedule (dates for pre-production, filming, editing, etc) will be devised by the producer or production manager, but you may be asked for your input. You will certainly be expected to be on top of the pre-production schedule – and you must not be personally responsible for it falling behind.

2. **Arrange travel and accommodation if necessary**
   This is usually a job for the production coordinator, but as budgets come down, so do team sizes, to reduce the number of people that need to be paid. This means many roles doubling up and researchers increasingly being asked to take on the role of production coordinator. (For tips on production coordination, see Chapter 4.)

3. **Order stock for filming**
   Again, this is usually someone else's job (the production manager), but it may end up in your lap – and if it does, make sure you do it well. Get enough of the right kind of stock. Turning up for a shoot with nothing to film on can be rather embarrassing, if not life-threatening.

4. **Arrange location agreements**
   Similarly, it's bad to turn up at a location only to be told that you are not allowed to film there. In the good old days, you'd go and film in a park and no questions would be asked. That is getting increasingly rare. Park wardens will stop you if you don't have the right paperwork. You even need permission to film on public streets these days. Make sure you organise it through the relevant authorities, and get appropriate documentation and a contact name and number, just in case a 'jobsworth' does come up and ask what you're doing.

5. Prepare consent forms

It's amazing to think we filmed 12 entire series of the hospital programme *Jimmy's* without one contributor release form being signed. In those days a verbal consent was enough – and our promise that patients, nurses and doctors could change their minds about being shown at any moment, even right up to transmission. But nowadays you need signed consent forms for contributors, locations, photos, videos and children. Children are a consent form minefield. Get parental releases if they're involved in any way, even non-speaking. Return to the office without all your signed release forms and you'll be in the bad books.

6. Make life easier for others

For example, at the top of the release form you could write a brief description of the person to whom it relates. The production manager will love you for that during programme clear-up.

7. Write impressive briefs for the presenter and producer

You will need good writing skills to be a researcher. After you've talked to your contributors and researched your locations, you'll be expected to write a succinct, accurate and informative brief. Poor spelling and waffle do not breed confidence. Don't rely on spellcheckers – if you're not very good at grammar, get a friendly colleague to check it through.

8. Be honest about your contributors

Put any doubts you have about the contributors into your research notes. If it all goes wrong during filming because they aren't very good, you can always say: 'Well, I told you so – and here's the proof!' (Saying 'I told you so' to your superior is normally career suicide, but it makes you feel better as you're being escorted out by security.)

9. Provide accurate information for the call sheets

Hopefully a production coordinator will be doing the call sheets, using the information you give them about times, locations, contributors and so on, but if the budget can't afford a production coordinator, you will be doing it (refer to Chapter 4 for tips on call sheets).

10. Check call sheets personally

Double-check that the call sheet has the right information and doesn't contain any typos. If telephone numbers, postcodes or timings are wrong, it will be you dealing with the fallout on location, not the production coordinator.

11. Remember to pack important stuff for filming

Depending on the nature of the shoot you may need to take a First Aid kit, a stills camera (for production stills), stationery, camcorder, refreshments, laptop and printer, etc. Don't think that remembering all of this is someone else's responsibility. Saying to a stressed-out director 'But I thought you were bringing the anti-venom!', as the presenter rolls round on the ground post-snake bite, will not go down well.

12. **Ring all the contributors the night before filming**

When I was a researcher, every time I forgot to do this (or was too busy), some disaster would ensue. One time we arrived at the location only to find that the contributors hadn't remembered that we were coming and had gone to the seaside. Another time, we got to the location and found the gates locked because the caretaker was ill. Always call people at the last minute to ensure they've remembered the filming and they are clear about the times and places to meet. This will help you get a good night's sleep.

Okay, the 'phoney war' is over – now it's on to the real thing … filming!

Filming: the researcher's role

Filming on location or in studio is where a researcher really proves their worth.

TWENTY THINGS YOU NEED TO DO WELL DURING FILMING TO BE A GREAT RESEARCHER

1. **Meet and greet contributors**

   If you're in a studio you should be one of the first faces they see. If you're on location you should be first out of the crew vehicle and first knocker on the door. You will already have a relationship with the contributors, so it should be you putting them at their ease, introducing them to the team and keeping them sweet as the crew sets up. Remember, it's very strange for ordinary people to have a group of strangers in their front room with loads of camera equipment. It's down to you to relax them.

2. **Help the shoot run smoothly**

   Time is precious on a filming day – and anything that wastes time causes stress. Do everything you can to make sure everything is organised to the nth degree.

3. **Keep morale up**

   Part of the researcher's role is to maintain morale. A couple of years ago I made a series for ITV called *Crash Scene Investigators*. It was about the police as they investigated serious car crashes. Not a fun subject. We were on call 24 hours a day. Most callouts were during the night. It was exhausting, and miserable at times, but the fact that the researcher was fun to be around, cracking jokes, doing impressions and keeping everyone's spirits up, made all the difference. Nothing drains a director's spirits more than seeing a researcher with a face like a broken zip.

4. **Foresee problems before they happen**

   Filming behind schedule and the lunchbreak's coming up? Offer to go on a sandwich run so that everyone's food is ready as soon as the director wants to break. Why wait for the director to suggest it? He's got enough to think about. Check that the director agrees, then get the sandwich order with a smile and a joke – the crew may have wanted a hot lunch and will need cheering up. Make sure that you get the presenter's order right. You need him to be in a good mood all afternoon!

5. Tick off the sequences on the shooting script

This will help you foresee problems and come up with solutions. For example, rain is forecast and you see that there is an exterior sequence to film later. Why not give the director the heads up about the forecast and ask him if he wants to do it now? If he agrees, do everything you can to make it happen, re-jig the filming schedule and spread the word so that everyone knows what is happening.

6. Be a link between crew and director

People in TV are often too focused on what they're doing to remember to talk to other people. A good researcher mitigates this by working as a link between the preoccupied director and the busy crew. If the crew members are about to revolt because they haven't had a meal break for six hours, have a quiet word with the director and let him know. Formulate a plan of action, then go and pacify the crew. Again, a smile and a joke goes a long way.

7. Think ahead

Shoots invariably fall behind. Stay in contact with the people you are due to film later in the day, so that if the shoot is running late, they won't assume you aren't coming and go down the pub. (This has happened to me several times.)

8. Think editorially

The content of the programme is part of a researcher's remit. Are the correct answers being achieved by the interviewer? Are the contributors delivering as you had hoped? Is the presenter 'getting' the programme? If the answer is 'No', what are you going to do about it? A well-timed suggestion to the director is always appreciated.

9. Label the rushes tapes properly

The tapes and their boxes should be clearly labelled with the date, programme title, content and a unique number. Properly labelled tapes make all the difference in post-production. The editor will love you forever – assuming you haven't wandered into the back of shot or can be heard chatting on the soundtrack! (Please note: throughout this book for 'tapes' read hard disks, optical disks, memory card, flash memory, etc – whatever storage media your camera uses.)

10. Take production stills on location

Photos of the contributors are often part of the deliverables (what the production company must send to the broadcaster after the programme's finished). Production stills are often overlooked because people are too busy. Not you though – you forget nothing!

11. Stay close to the action

It can be very irritating when something needs doing urgently and you can't track down your researcher. Keep near the director, then you can spring into action as soon as they ask you to do something.

12. Be authoritative

One reason that you're getting a researcher credit on the show rather than a runner credit is because you're expected to have sufficient experience and confidence to see off problems. If a cyclist is about to trundle straight through a shot that has taken ages to set up, what can you do? Perhaps you could politely head them off and ask them to wait a few minutes. Ask with a smile, and you'd be surprised how many people agree. I love it when my researchers care enough about the production to do things like that without being asked.

13. Take legible and useful notes

It helps enormously in the edit if someone is taking notes during a shoot. The best person to do that is usually the researcher. It might just be jotting down what is on each tape and any observations from the director. Or it may involve filling in log sheets – where you log the timecodes of the best answers and shots. By the way the 'Timecode' is a sequence of numbers which is invisibly burnt onto the tape – it's a bit like magic. The editor and cameraman can see these numbers, as can the director if he has a monitor (little TV) on set. For example:

Timecode 10.12.30.21
10 is hours – but this is normally adjusted to be the tape number
12 is minutes into the tape
30 is seconds
21 is frames (don't bother with this on your log sheets)

You may have to ask the cameraman for timecodes if there is no monitor. Work out with the cameraman early on how to do this in a way that causes the minimum amount of hassle.

14. Note the names of interviewees and their titles for the edit

This will help when the editor is doing the graphics for on-screen captions later. Check the spelling. People don't like it when you spell their name wrong on the telly, and they hate it if you get their title wrong. There's a big difference between 'inspector' and 'detective chief inspector'!

15. If you're interviewing on camera, get good answers!

Some producer/directors like their researcher to do the interviews with the contributors while they watch them on the monitor. If you are asked to be the interviewer you need to do a good job, as it can make or break the programme. (There are some tips on interviewing on camera in Chapter 9.)

16. Take good care of the rushes

Rushes are the most important things in TV. A tape with nothing on it is called 'stock'.

This can cost about £10. 'Rushes' are tapes with something on them. They can be priceless. Eg, footage of that rare snake you've spent 20 days trekking through the jungle to capture. The mum of the 12-year-old boy killed in a car crash, tearfully telling the story of what happened to her son. The police murder squad you've been following for six months finally arresting their prime suspect. If you lose a rushes tape which has this kind of irreplaceable material on it, you'll probably never forgive yourself. Your director certainly won't.

17. Have a system for the rushes

On the shoot, have somewhere special where you keep rushes. It should be separate from the stock to avoid confusion. And you need somewhere super safe back at the hotel. DVCAM rushes are small and memory cards even smaller. They are so easy to lose, it's terrifying – so do whatever you can to avoid it happening. For example, number tapes as soon as they come out of the camera. This will help you spot if one is missing.

18. Do your paperwork as soon as you get back to the hotel or office

Your job does not end once you've wrapped for the day. In the evening, log the expenses for that day, check your notes for the following day and make sure your release forms are in order. Call the producer/director to see if he needs anything. All this is best done as soon as you get back, rather than after you've all been down the pub!

19. Think about the editor

When you get back to base, make sure that the editor gets the rushes, filming notes and log sheets as soon as possible after the shoot – and if you have time, watch the edit for a while. It's a great way to learn.

20. Money money money ...

... is rarely sunny in a researcher's world. You are likely to be in charge of settling up the petty cash and expenses when you return to the office. This is particularly nightmarish on foreign shoots when you are dealing with other currencies. Hopefully you will have kept a detailed daily record to avoid drowning in undecipherable receipts!

There are situations where getting receipts can be problematic. A few years back I was on a documentary shoot where I had to pose undercover as a paedophile in the Far East (country's name withheld for legal reasons!). I was forking out loads of cash to pimps (to get access to the brothels), prostitutes (to get information about where the underage prostitutes were working) and policemen (bribes to stop them blackmailing me). Receipts were not an option. My expenses forms back at YTV were legendary. I think the accounts department framed them! Talking of which – now it's time for some foreign filming tips.

Filming abroad leads to unique challenges to researchers, which is why only experienced researchers usually get the trips. If you're a foreign filming 'virgin', read the section below. Then you can at least feel like you've been there, done it and blagged the T-shirt!

A PERSONAL VIEW

Foreign filming rocks. For me, there's no better feeling than flying into a country you've never visited before with someone else paying the bills. You're about to embark on an adventure where you'll meet remarkable people, go to amazing places and hear fascinating stories. All expenses paid. It doesn't get much better than that.

However, foreign filming does have its negatives. It's expensive, so you're expected to work long hours. It's stressful: foreigners often don't speak perfect English and sometimes they don't hit deadlines. It's nerve-wracking because a lot of responsibility is on your shoulders. Returning with a 'dog's breakfast' of a programme after spending all that money doesn't go down well with bosses…

Foreign filming can be tough – there's no doubt about it. I've had some dreadful experiences abroad.

Here are the top three in reverse order:

3. Enduring a massive argument with a presenter on a volcano in 40 degree heat. I was seven days into the worst diarrhoea episode ever known to man (or more precisely, to a man's behind). I'd had a heat rash down the entire left-hand side of my body for a month, and it was my birthday. And I lost the argument.

2. Narrowly surviving a life-endangering episode when a prostitute in an illegal brothel asked to borrow my pen (in reality, a secret microphone) while filming undercover in the Far East. Top tip to undercover journalists – always have a spare pen!

1. Sitting in my hotel room in Mumbai sensing tens of thousands of pounds of business slipping through my fingers. Terrorists were attacking nearby hotels, forcing the cancellation of the cricket tournament I was there to film. As I watched the news on TV, the bulletins predicted that my hotel might be attacked next. I was under room arrest and then disaster struck. I discovered the minibar was empty.

However, terrible experiences tend to make great anecdotes, and each of those three incidents turned out well in one way or the other, and that is what TV is all about – unpredictability. I've worked in more than 50 countries and met some truly wonderful people. Yusuf in Mumbai. Bob in Guam. Rolly in the Philippines. Anees in Bangalore. Simon in Indonesia. The list could go on, but I'd hate to embarrass them.

If you get a chance to film abroad, grasp it. It's an extreme version of what TV's all about.

FOREIGN FILMING: 14 TIPS FOR RESEARCHERS

1. **Take advice from other people**
   When you find out where you're going, pick the brains of other people who have worked there. Look into local customs. Start to get a feel for the country. For example, it's offensive to hand over money with your left hand in India – it's best to know that before you get there. You also need guidance on when to bribe and when not to bribe.

2. **Organise filming permits ASAP**
   You need all your permissions sorted before you fly anywhere, but sometimes this isn't possible. I spent a month on the phone in the UK trying to get permissions to film wildlife in India, and never made any progress. Eventually I had to gamble, fly out there and go to the government ministry in Delhi in person. I took an excellent local fixer and a box of cigarettes. Getting that permit from the national government to film wildlife was great. Then I found out I also needed permits from all the local governments and wildlife reserves. Cue four weeks trekking round offices in sweltering heat. The sensitivities and bureaucracy were unbelievable. I still don't know how we pulled it off.

3. **Sort the carnet**
   The carnet is the kit inventory that some countries require before they let you through customs. In an ideal world you can leave this to your production manager. If you do have to do it, don't miss anything out. You might not be able to bring it back to Britain with you!

4. **Arrange visas**
   Visas are often a source of stress. I almost didn't get into Dubai because my passport had an 'Israel' stamp in it. I nearly had my visa for the USA confiscated because the colleague I was travelling with was a Canadian without the requisite work permit. However, the closest shave I had was an Indian visa earlier this year. After weeks of waiting it finally came through, as I actually queued in the immigration office in London on my way to the airport.

5. **Get any immunisations you need in good time**
   The jabs can make you feel quite ill, so get them over with well in advance of filming. Make sure that the crew do this too.

6. **Book flights**
   If there is no production coordinator this could land in your lap, and it's an expensive thing to get wrong. Double-check dates. Make sure you aren't flying into a country on a public holiday. Make sure you've chosen the best airport from a logistical point of view. Try to do a deal on excess baggage, because you'll have lots of kit. One company I worked for was so obsessive about excess baggage fees that they insisted I travelled abroad with just 6lb of personal luggage. (That equated to about two pairs of underpants. I wear big pants.)

7. Don't forget your paperwork

You will need hard copies of all your filming permits (possibly in the local language). Also, you will need appearance releases, location releases and child releases – even for local tribespeople. You may be making your programme for an American broadcaster, and they're particularly strict about releases – no release, no show.

8. Important contacts

The contact details for the nearest hospital, embassy, lawyers, etc need to be on the call sheet, and the call sheet has to be triple-checked. Numbers for services such as Medevac (emergency assistance) need to be right.

9. Arrange vehicles

You need to sort crew vehicles in advance of departure, as this is much too important to try to do when you are out there. For example, I had difficulties finding crew vehicles that were big enough for all our kit in the Philippines. I eventually sourced two Pajeros. The only two in the entire nation. Within a week I'd personally crashed one into the other. Not my finest moment.

10. Organise power for battery charging

If you are filming in a jungle or desert, you will need a generator and fuel for it. They're generally quite noisy, bulky and prone to failure, so you might want to arrange two.

11. Find and negotiate a deal for local porters

You might need porters to help you carry stuff around. I know it sounds a bit colonial, but you try lugging 50 kit boxes around a jungle without some help.

12. Arrange reliable communication

Will you need a satellite phone? These can be erratic, but if you need Medevac quick, it's best not to rely on local mobiles.

13. Have a good time!

When you're filming abroad it's easy to get so stressed out that you forget what a great experience it is. One of my associate producers said that the favourite part of his day in our Far East wildlife shoot was when I started filming long time-lapse sequences. We would lock the camera off for half an hour and film the sunset, so that it could be speeded up in the edit. It was the only chance he had to sit down!

14. Bring a present back for your boss

It increases your chance of getting another foreign jaunt!

So there concludes the researcher chapter. You will also pick up research tips from reading other chapters in this book, as there are many areas of overlap. I strongly suggest you look at the production coordinator section in Chapter 4, and of course Chapter 6 (how to be a great associate producer) and Chapter 8 (producer/director tips), because that's where you're heading!

Photos: Snapshots From My Travels

South Africa 2009 – Some Rajasthan Royals cricketers I was filming for a DVD pose for a team photo. These players are international stars worshipped in India. Can you spot the odd man out?

South Africa 2007 – This photo was taken moments before the boat's motor ran out of fuel in a hippo and croc infested lagoon. The interviewee is explaining how a hippo can bite a man in half

Far East 1995 – My audition for the local version of *Britain's Got Talent* was going well until the presenter asked me my occupation. I couldn't say 'undercover reporter investigating the child sex trade'. I had to say 'paedophile'. They weren't impressed...

Best cure for arachnophobia – put a great big spider on your face and say cheese

The doctor said this was the worst case of piles he'd ever seen

Some researchers say monitor lizards like to eat small worms I reckon they prefer large snakes

The Full Monty – Krakatoa style. The locals actually paid us to put our clothes back on

India 2001 – Chameleons get anxious when held by humans, so I stroked this one to make it a calmer calmer calmer chameleon. Okay – weak joke, but can you think of a better one?!

India 2001 — South African fast bowler Morne Morkel is 6 foot 5 inches tall. I am 5 foot five and seven eighths — in my stocking feet. It made filming interviews with him something of a challenge

New York 2000 — This Discovery Channel award was for a documentary about controversial cosmetic surgery on children with Down's Syndrome. It's amazing how one phone call with a plastic surgeon about an unrelated topic can lead to a programme which generated headlines all over the world

India 2010 – South African cricket captain Graeme Smith told me he loved me and promised he'd give me an interview next day. He then broke his finger and flew home. What some people will do to avoid working with me

India 2001 – A king cobra bite injects enough venom to kill a small elephant in thirty minutes and an average-sized man in twenty minutes. I reckon I'd last about five seconds

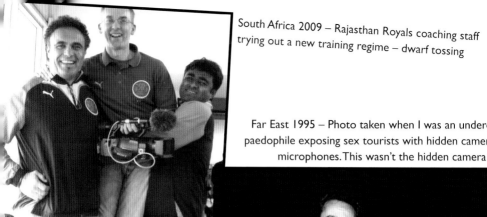

South Africa 2009 – Rajasthan Royals coaching staff trying out a new training regime – dwarf tossing

Far East 1995 – Photo taken when I was an undercover paedophile exposing sex tourists with hidden cameras and microphones. This wasn't the hidden camera

Scotland 2010 – Wearing a silly hat is de rigeur for directors. Legendary TV presenter Lorraine Kelly is trying not to laugh at mine

Australia 1999 – Photo taken during the filming of *Stunt School* (a series for the Discovery Channel). The car is about to skid across the road with a stunt rookie tied to the bonnet

Having survived the skidding car stunt, the stunt rookie is now involved in a near miss with a motorbike. I guess it is what you call 'having a bad day at the office'

I direct from a safe distance – if it all goes wrong I don't want my nice hat to get covered in stunt rookie body parts

Australia 1999 – My audition for the Robin role on the next *Batman* movie ended in tears. I refused to wear my underpants outside my trousers

Australia 2009 – I flew all the way to Australia just to interview world-famous cricketer Shane Warne. The first thing he said to me was 'Sorry mate, I've broken my tooth. Gotta go to the dentists'. He was still one of the most articulate interviewees I've ever filmed

Chapter 6:
How To Be A
Great Shooting
Associate Producer

Chapter 6: How To Be A Great Shooting Associate Producer

Being an associate producer (or assistant producer, if you're at the BBC) is often the next step on the career ladder after being a researcher. It requires many of the same skills in terms of story, people and location finding, but there are some crucial differences. One is that, with the enhanced credit comes enhanced responsibility. You may be expected to direct second unit (where you go off with a second cameraman to film additional material). You may even be expected to direct the main camera if the director is ill or indisposed.

Generally, you will also be expected to be able to film your own material with a smaller camera (a Sony Z1, for example). Shooting your own stuff is tough. No doubt about it. Whether it's your first time or whether you've been doing it for years, shooting programme content solo is a big 'ask'. You're combining the roles of cameraman, sound recordist, researcher, spark, director and producer. It's practically impossible to do all those things perfectly on your own, but when do you pull it off it's very rewarding – you can justifiably say that part of the programme is all yours.

Many things can go wrong because you're multi-skilling so much. The main way to avoid errors is not to rush. If you take your time, you're less likely to forget to press the record button, fail to switch the radio mic on, overexpose everything or make any of the other hundred or so mistakes that can easily occur.

However, it's not just about avoiding 'cock-ups'. At all times you should be endeavouring to enhance the production value of your programme. Just because you're on your own doesn't mean you can't come back with impressive content.

Your aim is for the editor to be willing to talk to you after he's cut your footage. That is a good sign: it means that he hasn't had to slave over making a silk purse sequence out of your sow's ear rushes! You should still ask his advice about what you could have done differently, though. Editors appreciate the input and their suggestions are always spot on.

Good luck – and happy shooting!

Learning the basics

The tips in this chapter assume that you already have some knowledge of filming and how to operate a basic camera. If you don't have any shooting experience, get some. Buy or borrow a camera. Even if it's just a domestic camcorder, get used to the buttons and film and edit videos for YouTube. Then, try to graduate to a proper industry camera. Most learning establishments and all production companies have decent cameras lying around. Get some tips (or even better, come on one of my training courses), then get as much practice as you can, as quickly as you can.

Let's assume you've been through this process and know which way to point a camera. You've probably done some hard yards as a researcher and you've graduated to an associate producer position. Before long, you'll probably be asked to go and film something. It's your big chance. Here are some tips on how to avoid blowing it. First of all, as with most things in TV, preparation is critically important.

BEFORE YOU GO FILMING: EIGHT TOP TIPS

1. Have a good 'play' with the camera in the office

A good ploy is to say to the production manager that you want to 'tech check' the kit. In reality, you're reminding yourself how to use it – but they don't need to know that! (There's no need for your credibility to take a hit because you're being sensible – TV is all about perceptions.) Set the camera up and film something in the office. Are the menu settings to your satisfaction? Are you getting sound and vision on tape? Play it back to check. This is the best time to find out that something isn't working. It's better trying to work out what's wrong the night before your shoot, rather than in front of your nervous contributors – or impatient presenter!

2. Become familiar with the tripod

Tripods are essential for many shots, but they can be a nightmare to set up if you are not used to them. Think about your dad trying to put up a deckchair on the beach – painful to watch. Have a good practice setting up your tripod and taking it down before you use it.

3. Don't be lazy

Don't be tempted to think 'That tripod's a bit heavy. I might accidentally leave it behind.' If you do this, some of your shots will look wobbly and amateurish. Why not suggest that the company buys a lightweight tripod instead? They are only £50 and usually fit for purpose.

4. It's all about the lighting

As a director friend said to me when I first started out, 'It's all about the lighting'. Before you go to film an interior shoot, ask your production manager if you can take a powerful light with you. A 'blonde' is easy to use: it will make your shots look much better. Bounce the light off the ceiling – don't point it directly at the subject. If you're filming outdoors at night or in a dark corridor, ask the production manager for a camera-top light. There are some really handy LitePanel lights available these days if you need to persuade your production manager to buy one.

5. Make sure you can get the radio mics to work

Again, check them the night before. Radio mics can be quite fiddly. If they're not working, don't panic, as it is normally the batteries, or you're confusing the transmitter with the receiver, or they're on different frequencies. If you can't figure it out, ask someone. Make sure you do your rehearsal while someone is around who can help you if you get stuck – not at midnight.

6. Get a good night's sleep

Being a shooting associate producer is hard work, both physically and mentally. Make sure you're well rested before you do it – or as well rested as you can be in the middle of a hectic filming schedule!

7. Do a shooting script

Never set foot outside the office without thinking carefully about what you're going to shoot and how you're going to shoot it. Do a shooting script, where you map out how you expect the final piece to look and the shots you'll need to cover commentary. You should still be flexible to developments on the shoot itself, but having a wish list and a structure in advance will help you avoid forgetting obvious shots such as general views (GVs) and introduction shots (see the shooting script template in Chapter 8 on page 126).

8. Fully charge your batteries

A camera needs batteries to operate. There is nothing worse than seeing your battery power and filming time dwindle away. It happened to me in New Caledonia and resulted in us missing the capture of a rare giant gecko. The presenter was furious. As shooting associate producer, you are responsible for making sure that your batteries are fully charged. Set up a charging station at home (or at your hotel), and charge batteries overnight, every night. Bear in mind that batteries have a shorter lifespan in the cold. Hug them to keep them warm and show them that you love them.

Old timer's tip: when filming abroad, take a four-way adaptor and just one continental adaptor. Plug all your kit into the four-way, and use the adaptor for the four-way plug. It saves money.

So, you've done all your pre-shoot preparations and you're ready to spring into action. Now it's time to go and film. The shooting associate producer role really is the epitome of multi-skilling. These are the roles you need to fulfil: cameraman, sound recordist, spark, director and producer. Let's go through them one by one and give you some guidance on how to do each role well.

The cameraman role

This role is obviously hard to forget because you're physically holding the camera, but there is a lot to think about when it comes to getting good shots...

20 TOP CAMERA TIPS

1. Don't get your kit stolen before you start!

Keep your precious camera close and visible. A colleague of mine left her Sony Z1 camera on the floor in a fast food restaurant in London. One minute it was there, the next it was gone, and she hadn't even shot a frame. It should have been on the table. There's less risk of it being stolen.

2. Keep your kit safe from the environment

Watch out for dust, sand, water and dirt – eg, don't put your camera or tapes down on a beach. I made that mistake once, and there were horrible glitches all over the footage because grains of sand had got to the tapes. Also, always use a cover to protect your camera from the rain.

3. Check your white balance

Cameras don't know precisely what is white – this is where white balance comes in. Some cameras have buttons for this: indoor, outdoor settings, etc. Other cameras try to work out white (and hence all the other colours) automatically. Some allow you to set it manually by using a piece of white card. This matters because not all light is the same colour. Sunlight is blue-ish and artificial light (such as lightbulbs) is orange-ish. Your eyes and brain can process this information naturally, but the camera tends to make everything look all one colour if it's on the wrong setting. If it looks wrong in the viewfinder, you need to alter the white balance.

4. Don't rush

You must not start until you are totally ready – and I mean, 100 per cent ready. It's easy to rush when you're inexperienced and you don't want to hold important people up. But if you do rush, you're likely to forget something important. Perhaps the radio mic is on the table instead of being fixed to the interviewee's tie? Perhaps the top mic cable isn't fully inserted into the camera? Or perhaps the shot isn't totally level because the tripod is wonky? These have all happened to me when I've been rushing to complete a shoot. Take your time, and cover all your bases.

5. Remember to switch on the record button

This may seem obvious, but it can be forgotten. I once filmed an extremely emotional interview with a couple who had lost a son in a car accident. I was asking the questions and the shooting associate producer was filming. It was a very powerful interview: the couple were very tearful and articulate about their loss, but halfway through I heard the camera shut down. This meant that the camera had been doing nothing for 10 minutes. The shooting associate producer had forgotten to press the record button. Absolute nightmare: we had to start again, and it took a long time to get any emotion second time around. We couldn't give up – the couple would have seemed cold in the final programme if they hadn't cried about their loss – but it was still extremely uncomfortable. One of the worst experiences of my career.

6. Do an early technical check

As soon as possible into your shoot, make sure that you are getting good sound and pictures on to the tape. The best way to do this is by pressing the record review button. This plays the last few seconds back to you and doesn't create a break in the timecode. If there's a fault with the camera (or you), it's best to know 10 minutes into the shoot, not two weeks later when it gets to edit.

7. Take your time composing your shots

It comes more naturally to some than to others, but make sure that you don't begin recording until your frame looks perfect. If in doubt, shoot slightly wider – the editor can zoom in and readjust, using the edit software if necessary. They can't zoom out if you're too tight.

8. Remember 'head room' when framing

If it looks like there is a lot of space above a person's head in your frame, then you've got too much 'headroom'. My personal preference when it comes to headroom is a close-up, with the top of the head just touching the top of frame. Don't cut the head in half – that would be too little headroom!

9. Remember 'eye room' too

There should be more distance in the frame in the direction where the interviewee is looking compared to behind them. So, if they're looking left to right at the interviewer, there should be more room to the right of the frame. That's called eye room. You don't position people dead centre unless they're doing a piece to camera.

10. Always record five seconds before and after the shot you want.

Editing decks need run 'up time' to synchronise the timecode, and they struggle without enough pre-roll. So, start recording, then cue the action five seconds later. And when the action finishes, wait five seconds before you stop recording. This means the editor has the option of holding the shot for a few extra seconds at the end.

11. Avoid autofocus

In autofocus mode the camera often searches for a sharp focus when you least want it to, and this leads to soft shots. Focus manually by going through the following process:

1. Switch the camera to manual focus
2. Zoom in fully tight to some detail, usually teeth or eyebrows if it's a human face
3. Focus on the detail, and then zoom out to your composed shot. The detail (and hence the face) will still be in focus.

12. Auto iris

In my opinion the auto iris feature is acceptable if you really have your hands full. But if you have time, manually control your iris – then your exposure won't fluctuate when you don't want it to.

13. The auto sound settings on most cameras are pretty good

I've had less pain using the auto sound settings than the manual sound settings, which are easily knocked.

14. SOS: Stay On Shots!

It's very hard to edit a sequence if the camera never settles. Find a good frame, and stay with it. Let the action happen within that frame.

15. Don't 'twitch' the shot

This really annoys editors. They see a nice shot in the rushes, start to cut it into the sequence and just before the shot is long enough, the cameraman twitches the iris or focus because it isn't quite right. You're better sticking with it, or if you're not sure, starting all over again. Regular adjustments to your shots just as you're settling are a sign of inexperience. You want to give the impression that you're an expert if you want more work!

16. Use the 'legs' as much as possible

There are some easy things you can do to improve the production value of your shots. One is get the camera on the tripod as much as possible, especially for interviews and GVs (general views of houses, countryside, buildings, etc). The editor may hold these shots for 10 seconds, so they need to be steady. If you're running round after a police team making arrests, then obviously it has to be hand-held, but if you have chance to compose a shot and get it steady by using the tripod then you should do so. If people want shaky camerawork, they can watch YouTube.

17. Don't 'wave the camera around'

If you're filming a rapid conversation, don't try to film every talking head or you'll end up 'waving the camera around' and it'll be hard to cut. The editor needs static shots to edit the sequence (see tip number 14). If it's a more sedate conversation then by all means try to film all the talking heads, but make sure that you set up listening shots at the end to cover the camera moves.

18. Try to get 'separation' between the subject and background and 'dress' the frame

Eg, don't have an interviewee backed up against a wall. 'Separation' involves getting them away from the background, which means that you can have the subject in focus and the background slightly soft, which looks better. Bricks aren't all that interesting and white walls are generally dirty. And remember, you can dress the background. Move a plant, adjust the practical anglepoise lamp, maybe add some books? You're in control. Make an effort, so that the whole frame looks as good as possible.

19. Avoid things coming out of the top of people's heads

You should remove distracting objects from the background. Someone with a cactus coming out of the top of their head is not good. Move the camera. Or them. Or the cactus.

20. Think of the content when deciding the size of your frame

I once shot a really emotional interview in a mid-shot because the background was quite pretty. It was a big mistake. The emotion needed close-ups. I got a justifiable telling off when I got back to the office. Stick to mid-close-ups, close-ups and big close-ups if you are shooting emotional content, but please don't zoom into tears – it's so 1970s!

So, there were some camera tips to get you started. However, there's more to the shooting associate producer role than just operating the camera. If you're self-shooting, you are also the sound recordist.

EIGHT TOP SOUND TIPS

1. **Use good mics**
   Never use the internal camera mic, it's rubbish. Try to get a decent top mic and good specification radio mics.

2. **Wear headphones so that you can monitor sound**
   Radio mic batteries run out quite quickly. With headphones on you are more likely to notice sound problems – like the radio mics failing, or wind rustle on the top mic.

3. **Use both audio tracks**
   Most tapes have two audio tracks. It's best to use them both to give the editor options in the edit. The radio mic can go on one track, the camera top mic on the other.

4. **Use status check on your camera**
   Use the status check on your camera to ensure you are getting sound on both audio tracks. If one of your leads isn't working, status check will show that the levels aren't moving for the mic on that track.

5. **Have a system!**
   I always put the radio mic on track 1 and the camera top mic on track 2. This means that the 'phantom' power settings (the switches on the front of the camera) are always right. It also means that I know what mic is on which track when I'm editing.

6. **Point the camera (and top mic) away from noisy backgrounds**
   Instead of interviewing someone with their back to a busy road, move them so that they have their back to a nice quiet park – assuming, of course, that the interview isn't about excessive traffic noise! The top mic is directional – it will pick up sound from whatever direction it is pointing.

7. **Protect your radio mic from wind**
   Radio mics need little 'wind gags'. Don't forget to put them on. You should also try to get your interviewee to face away from the wind, so that their body shields the mic a bit too.

8. **Beware of music**
   If you can hear music, get it turned off or go somewhere else. Music all over the soundtrack makes it uneditable.

The strategies for recording sound differ according to the type of sequences you are filming...

SOUND SUGGESTIONS FOR DIFFERENT FILMING SCENARIOS

An interview where you ask questions which will be edited out of the final programme

Put a radio mic on the interviewee: somewhere it won't rub, and not too close to their mouth or it will keep 'popping'. It should be on the side they are facing. The best position is three inches above sternum height (or above nipple height, if you don't know what the sternum is!). The radio mic should not be too obtrusive. You can also have the top mic running as a safety, but you probably won't use it because it is further away from the sound source, so the sound won't be as good.

An interview where someone asks questions which might be used in the final programme

The top mic is very directional and isn't much help for hearing the interviewer, as it will be pointing at the interviewee. So try to get your hands on two radio mics and mic up both talkers. Alternatively, get a hand mic for the interviewer and put that on channel 2 instead of the top mic.

A meeting where a number of people are talking and you need to record all of them

The main talker must wear a radio mic. Other contributors should be 'poled' whenever possible: this involves putting a mic on the end of a sound pole and getting an assistant to point it at whoever is talking. If this isn't possible, use the camera top mic on track 2, but beware: for best results you need to be close to the talkers and pointing the camera at them when they're talking. Not easy.

Filming actuality where there is lots of movement and lots of people talking

For example, a police drugs bust or patients being treated in an Accident & Emergency Department. Try to get a radio mic on your main talker. Get the rest of the talkers on the top mic and bear in mind that the closer you are, the better you'll hear someone. But always remember the needs of the people you're filming. There is no point getting so close to the action that you put the paramedic off and they refuse to let you film anymore. If someone says a great line and you miss it because you're pointing the camera in the wrong direction, you can try to get them to say it again at the end. It probably won't work in the edit (they're not actors), but there is no harm in trying!

Hopefully you will find these sound tips useful. Bad sound is often the hardest thing to rescue in the edit. You have been warned! Now on to another thing for you to think about if you're a shooting associate producer – lighting.

HOW TO LIGHT LIKE THE PROFESSIONALS: FIVE TOP TIPS

1. **You should have brought some lights from base, so use them!**
   It doesn't have to be a dark room for lights to improve your shots significantly. Use all the lights at your disposal effectively.

2. **Take your time**
   Don't rush. Use all your lights and 'practicals' (ie, existing lighting) if you need to. Ideally you will have three lights. The key light (the main one lighting the face), the fill light (lighting the other side of the face) and the back light (adding light to the back of the head). Once you've lit the subject, have a look at the shot in the viewfinder – you'll see the difference.

3. **Try to light up your subject's eyes**
   If you can get light into the eyes they often come up beautifully. The contributor will thank you when they see the programme go out.

4. **Separate the subject from the background**
   If you've placed the subject away from the background, like you should have done, you may be able to light them so that they are well lit and the background is slightly darker. That can look really nice.

5. **Avoid 'silhouetting' subjects**
   People often complain about the lights blinding them, but that's the way it has to be. You want light to go into the face because the face is what the viewer wants to see. Never shoot against a bright window so the face is shadowed. Auto iris would expose for the window, giving the interview a 'film noir' feel that you probably don't want. Unless of course your interviewee is part of a witness protection programme!

Being the camera operator, the sound recordist and the spark may sound like a lot but there's even more to the shooting assistant producer's role. You're also the director, in charge of the look of the piece.

12 TOP TIPS

1. **You're the director – act like it!**
    Take charge, be authoritative. This breeds respect and confidence in the people you are filming.

2. **Have a strict routine**
    There is so much to think about when you're a shooting associate producer and there is a lot to forget. Give yourself every chance of remembering everything by having a strict routine. Mine for an interview is as follows:

    * Say hello and warm up the contributor
    * Check out the location
    * Decide where to film. Set up chairs – yours and theirs
    * Tripod up
    * Camera on tripod, level it
    * Battery on
    * Tape in
    * Get pictures sorted – find a nice frame
    * Get sound sorted – check that the radio mic is working. Put it on their chair
    * Get the contributor in
    * Put the radio mic on them. You can't forget – it's on their chair!
    * Find a nicer frame, now that the contributor is sitting down
    * Keep chatting while you do final adjustments. Is the contributor warmed up?
    * Double-check that you're getting sound and pictures
    * Talk up the contributor a bit more
    * Record

    Do this routine often enough and you're more likely to notice if you've missed something out.

3. **Use the words 'action' and 'cut'**
    You might feel a bit of a pillock saying 'action' and 'cut' when you first start out, but those words exist in TV for good reason. They help everyone know what's going on: is the camera running? Yes, if the director has said 'action'. Has the camera stopped? Yes, if the director has said 'cut'. Using the words 'action' and 'cut' also establishes to everyone around you that: (1) you're experienced; (2) you've been well trained; or (3) you've read this book (delete as appropriate). All good things.

4. **Remember you're filming 'sequences'**

   You aren't just filming shots. You're filming shots that will be put together by the editor to make sequences for the programme. For example, start with a geography/establisher shot…

5. **Geography/establisher shot**

   The first shot of a sequence is generally a wide shot, so that the viewer can see who is there, the direction that they're facing and what they're doing. This shot may also be needed for commentary to explain what's happening. The editor will then cut to tight shots and the action, but before that the viewer needs to get a sense of geography. That is down to you.

6. **Get cutaways**

   Your editor won't forgive you returning without cutaways, because he won't be able to edit the sequence. A cutaway often used in interviews is the 'close-up noddie': this is simply someone listening and nodding. A useful cutaway in an actuality sequence is a 'watching shot'. If a policeman is arresting someone, it's wise to get a five-second shot of someone watching. Then the editor can reduce down the 10 minutes it took to put on the handcuffs to two seconds, by cutting to the watcher and then back to the 'crim' being led off to the slammer.

7. **Get 'wallpaper' shots**

   These are shots which can be used for 'thought track', commentary and music sequences. Three examples: parents playing with their kids in a park, a bereaved family laying flowers at a graveside, the family of a person who's missing abroad looking out to sea. The editor can use these shots under sound from the interviews, musical interludes and the programme voice over. Documentaries chew up sequences like this. The more you get, the better.

8. **Be creative**

   Make sure you get 'bookend' shots to get you in and out of a sequence: a typical 'get in' shot is a wide of the action, and a typical 'get out' shot is a low angle of people walking away from camera. The more you think about each shot and how you can make it as pretty as possible, the more fun you'll have – and the more you'll be noticed by people who may want to promote you.

9. **Be sensible about your shots**

   I was doing an interview once and, unbeknown to me, the shooting associate producer who was filming it wasn't on the face of the person I was talking to – oh no, that would have been too obvious. He was roving up and down their face and body. I couldn't believe it when I got back to the edit suite. His shots were totally unusable. I hadn't even asked him to be avant garde. He just decided to do it. Unbelievable.

10. Don't 'sit on the wide'

When they first start out, a lot of people will just keep filming the wide shot to make sure that they don't miss anything. They're too scared to get cutaways. This makes the sequence uneditable; plus it looks bad if someone is emotional and there is no close up.

11. Don't cut too quick

Leave a pause after you think you've got enough. Then say 'Cut', pause again, and then switch off the record button. Editors like long holds at the end of sequences, and many inexperienced cameramen cut the camera too quick.

12. Shoot loads!

It's good to have lots of options in the edit, so shoot everything that moves. If the editor moans about too much material, then give him the timecodes of the best bits, so he doesn't have to wade through all the rubbish.

So, there were some tips for the director side of being a shooting associate producer. You may want a breather and a lie down by now, but there's one more role to discuss. You're also the producer. As director you're in charge of the visuals, and as producer you're in charge of the content. Here are some tips on how to get good content.

The producer role

EIGHT TOP TIPS

1. Do you need emotion?

Do you need tears for the story to work? If so, what is the question or scene that will get you the emotion you want? This may seem cynical, but it's the way TV operates. You can't tell an emotional story and engage the TV audience enough for them to care without actually seeing emotion (usually tears) on camera. There are certain trigger questions that interviewers can ask to get emotion, for example:

Go back to the moment when you found out what had happened – tell me how you felt. What did you tell your kids?
How are your kids coping – it must break your heart seeing them so upset?

Making people cry isn't something I enjoy doing, but it can be part of the job (and I've been told by counsellors that having a good cry can do everyone good from time to time). However, you may need a totally different feel from your interview…

2. **Do you need humour?**

   If so, let the contributors know. They'll often deliver if they know you want laughs. But first you need to create an upbeat vibe in the room. Crack a few jokes yourself to get them into the mood. One tip though: if you feel the need to laugh, leave a pause after their punchlines. Then the editor has the option of editing your laugh out or tightening it up and keeping it in. Alternatively…

3. **Do you want conflict?**

   If so, set it up, light the blue touchpaper, step back and film the conflagration. Make sure you have a fresh tape and battery, because you may only get it once. Quite a few recent observational documentary programmes have thrived on creating conflict – it does generate good viewing figures. (Mentioning no names, but one producer did put four cans of lager in a former alcoholic's fridge, knowing it would lead to his wife going ballistic!)

4. **Decide what you want from your shoot and keep going until you get it**

   There is no point going to all this effort and not getting the best content you possibly can. Rookies tend not to film enough.

5. **Don't be afraid to retake**

   Tape is cheap. If you think you can get better content by doing it again, don't be shy – feel free to suggest a retake or two. But don't overdo it. The law of diminishing returns does set in fairly rapidly and you need to keep your contributors sweet. You may want to film them again one day.

6. **Label tapes properly**

   As producer, if you are working solo, you are also in charge of boring stuff such as labelling tapes and boxes because there is no researcher around to delegate it to. Do it carefully – it reduces the risk of losing rushes and makes life easier for the editor.

7. **Make sure you don't leave rushes tapes behind**

   A friend of mine (who shall remain nameless) left a bag full of DVCAM rushes on a plane coming back from South America. They were never seen again. Miraculously the executive producer didn't notice!

8. **After the shoot, convert the shooting script into an edit script**

   Part of the producer's role is seeing the project through the edit. The sooner you adjust your shooting script to what actually happened on location, the better (a shooting script/ edit script template is discussed in chapter 8 on page 126). Do these adjustments while the shoot is still fresh in your memory, then view your rushes and add timecodes to make it into an edit script. Delivering an edit script to the editor means that your creative vision is more likely to be realised, even if you're unable to be there during the edit. The editor will be grateful that he hasn't just been handed a load of rushes and asked to get on with it!

So there you have the inside track on the shooting associate producer's role. So far I've focused mainly on filming interviews, because that will be the bulk of what you are asked to do. Filming actuality (people actually doing things) is much more challenging. Consequently, it warrants a section of its own...

Filming actuality sequences

A PERSONAL VIEW

Filming interviews when you're self shooting is relatively straightforward. You sit down (or stand up) and your interviewee sits down (or stands up). It's usually best if you both do the same. (Unless they're very tall and you're very short – like me interviewing 6ft 5in South African cricketer Morne Morkel.)

Then you point the camera at the interviewee, check you're getting sound, frame it as nicely as you can and start asking questions. You occasionally glance at the viewfinder to make sure they're still in frame, but most of the time you maintain eye contact with your interviewee, so that they feel you're interested in what they're saying.

There is a lot to think about when filming interviews solo, but compared to filming actuality, interviews are a walk in the park. Actuality sequences are a real challenge. Filming things like policemen arresting people or paramedics saving someone's life is tough because you need to film all the important bits, you can't get people to do things again and you need to get cutaways while it's all happening. If you get in the way and upset someone, you can screw up your access. It's not easy – but if you get it right, it's a great feeling.

Filming actuality: the principles

- You need a wide geography shot at the top of the sequence
- You need to capture the important bits on tape
- You need to be able to edit it, so you must get cutaways
- You need a shot to get you out of the sequence.

Filming actuality: the practice

It all boils down to the following question:
Can you control the situation that you're filming? The more control you have, the easier it is to film.

There are three categories of actuality situations when it comes to 'controllability':

1. Controllable situations – for example, someone making a cup of tea or feeding ducks in a pond. It's controllable because you decide when and where they start, where they finish and what they do.
2. Semi-controllable situations – for example, filming a business meeting or dinner party. You have some control over when they start, but once it has started and it is happening, you need to leave them to it in order to get realistic content.
3. Non-controllable situations – for example, filming the police as they arrest someone or a surgeon conducting an operation. You have no control whatsoever. You have to shoot what you can as it happens.

TIPS FOR THESE THREE SCENARIOS

1. **Filming a controllable situation**
   This is relatively easy, but still requires a strategy to get the best results. This is the strategy I follow in controllable situations:

   1. Action – think about the action you want and rehearse it in your head
   2. Organise – then organise it. Explain the action clearly to everyone
   3. Master – get the master wide sequence of the action
   4. Tight pick-ups – then do it all again to get tight shots of bits of the action
   5. Art – think art if you can. It could win you a BAFTA! Eg, top shots and low angles
   6. 'Bookend shots' – remember to film shots to get you in and out of the sequence.

   Let's apply this strategy to a 'walking in the park and feeding ducks' sequence:

   1. Action – work out where you want them to start walking from and where you want them to get to before they feed the ducks. Remember, you're in charge!
   2. Organise – explain to all the contributors what you need them to do. Talk them through it at least twice. If necessary, walk it through yourself while they watch, then there's a slim chance they'll do what you want them to do.
   3. Master – film a wide shot of them doing the whole thing. The walk up. The stop. Feeding the ducks for a while. Then the walk off in the direction of your choosing. This is the master shot. It's your safety, so get it right.
   4. Tight pick-ups – get them to do the whole thing again. This time, get some close-ups and different angles. Stop and start them. 'Can you walk past camera a few times?' 'Can you throw the bread just there so I can get a tight shot of it landing in the water?' 'Can you put your arm round him like you did before?' Remember, you always have the master shot to go back to in the edit.
   5. Art – is there a big wide top shot you can get of them feeding the ducks? Try to find a rooftop overlooking the lake, or stand on a nearby transit van – ideally with the owner's permission! Will that give the impression that they're small and insignificant in

the grand scheme of things? That might be good. Or maybe it's just a nice shot. Whatever – don't just go for the obvious.

6. 'Bookend shots' – a useful opening shot is the contributors walking towards camera and leaving frame. The fact that they leave frame means that you can cut straight to the duck feeding at the pond. A closing shot I often get is a low-angle leaving shot. Put the camera on the ground and get the contributors to enter frame and walk away from camera. I can almost hear the sad music as you go to the commercial break!

2. **Filming a semi-controllable situation, for example, a business meeting**
In this sort of situation you know the contributors won't start until you say 'Action', but after that there's no stopping them. Here's a suggested strategy for filming a meeting:

1. Make sure you have a new tape and full battery
2. Get there in good time. Arrange the chairs so that the set-up suits you. You need at least one empty chair to give you space to film through
3. Light the whole area if you can
4. When the contributors arrive, explain clearly what you need and ask them politely not to start until you say 'Action'. Check that everyone is happy to be filmed
5. When you're ready, start recording, then say 'Action'
6. Get the geography wide shot for 30 seconds or so
7. Then get tighter shots of the main talkers as they make their points
8. Don't wave the camera around! Settle on shots
9. If you miss an important point, don't stress – just try to remember what it was
10. When you have enough usable content for your programme, pick up 'internal cutaways' for the edit. These are listening shots, big wides, shots through doorways, shots from outside, etc
11. When the meeting is finished, switch on the charm and ask if some people can stay behind to do 'pick-ups'
12. 'Pick-ups' are important questions or answers you missed because you were pointing the camera in the wrong direction. It's worth trying to get them again after the meeting – sometimes they work in the edit.

3. **Filming a non-controllable situation. Eg, the police arriving at a car crash**
These scenarios are the most difficult to shoot. This is my suggested strategy:

Try to travel with the police to the crash scene in their car

Get lots of shots from inside the car: driver's face, hands on the steering wheel, shots through the front windscreen, gear changes, etc. You'll hopefully get some useful content on the way too. If you have a good relationship with the police, they may talk about the incident they're going to in a way that the viewers will understand.

My top tips for in-car filming: try to get in the passenger seat if you can. However, it's more likely that you'll need to be in the back so the police officers can be in the front. Ask to remove the headrests so you can get a better shot. You'll be very wobbly because the car will be going fast. So try to wedge the camera against the roof to give it some stability.

Get your arrival shot the moment you arrive

When you get there, jump out of the car and sprint as far away from the police officers as you can. Then swing the camera around and get shots of them walking towards the scene of the accident. It will help the editor if they leave frame in this shot – it means he can cut to them anywhere at the scene.

Tip for filming crime scenes: don't trample on the evidence!

Film the action

Film wider shots than you normally would because you can't anticipate what is going to happen. The more experience you have, the easier it is to predict what's going to happen next: for example, at what stage a casualty is usually put into an ambulance. This helps you get into position to film it.

Tip for getting steady hand-held shots: wedge your right elbow into your chest to help support the camera, or rest your elbow on a wall.

Get 'internal' cutaways

These are shots that you get during the action which will help in the edit, eg, someone watching what's happening. Ideally this would be someone relevant, perhaps a relative of the casualty, but be careful about upsetting people. You don't want to screw up your access to the police unit by inviting a complaint about your insensitivity.

Tips for internal cutaways: if you spot a good cutaway shot, try to get three sizes: wide, mid-shot and close up. Hold each for five seconds. Hey presto – three usable cutaways in 15 seconds. Now get back on to the action!

Don't wave the camera around

Let the action happen within the frame. If you try to film everything and never hold the camera steady, the footage will be uneditable.

Try to get usable moves

A pan from the police car with the flashing 'blues and twos' (lights and sirens) to the smashed-up car might work, but it can't be too long or it won't make the show, and if it's too quick the shot won't be usable either. Steady as she goes!

Tips for pans: hold both ends of a pan for a good five seconds. Then, even if the pan is useless, the editor can use the shots at either end.

Try to make the scenario 'semi-controllable' at the end

Once all the action has happened and the police have done their duty, you may be able to extract some favours from them. They may pretend to arrive again so that you can get a tight shot of them getting out of the car. Or they'll help you get a nice closing shot by waiting for your cue before getting into their car and driving off. It can make all the difference to your sequence – well worth a pint at the Policeman's Ball!

So there you have it – the world of the shooting associate producer and some tips on how to do it well.

Please note: there are big crossover skills with researchers (one step below you on the career ladder) and producer/directors (one level above), so I suggest you read those chapters too.

Chapter 7:
Development Team
Skills

Chapter 7: Development Team Skills

Development is the process of thinking up new TV programmes and trying to get them commissioned by broadcasters. I've worked in development at various stages of my TV career and I think it's a bit like America: a nice place to visit, but you wouldn't want to live there. Some call it 'development hell'. This is because you're not actually making programmes. You spend most of your time stuck in an office just thinking, and it's very frustrating seeing so many ideas rejected. Personally, I think the word 'hell' is too strong a word for it; perhaps 'limbo' is better. The regular wait for feedback from broadcasters can seem like an eternity.

Some people love being in development. It certainly has its appeals. Creating an idea that gets commissioned is a tremendous buzz and can be extremely lucrative. Imagine coming up with *Who Wants To Be A Millionaire?* or *The Weakest Link* – inventing a format that is sold all over the world can make you very rich.

Pitching ideas to broadcasters can be fun too. It's a stressful yet exciting process. As a former colleague once said to me, there's no better feeling than drinking a gin and tonic on the train back up north after having a programme commissioned. Plus you often get the chance to work on the programme, so it means you have guaranteed work for a few months – an added bonus.

One facet of pitching ideas is that you tend to promise the earth to get a commission. 'Talking cows? Yeah, no problem.' 'Access to NASA's manned voyage to Mars? Sure!' Then it's down to the poor producer to deliver what has been offered, and watch the broadcaster die a little bit when they see it for the first time. I've been on both sides of this particular conundrum. People do 'over-promise' with the best intentions – trying to get TV programmes made and keep their friends, colleagues and themselves in work. But these best intentions can lead to a lot of pain for the actual programme makers.

Development is a hard nut to crack. I've worked in a variety of companies with widely contrasting approaches. From one person beavering away on their own to large teams brainstorming ideas daily; from months spent slaving away on one idea to a more scattergun '20 one liners to a friendly commissioner' approach.

Please note the 'friendly commissioner' in that last sentence. A personal relationship with the person you're selling to is very helpful. Perhaps it's understandable: people like to work with people they like.

Be that as it may, if you come up with a fantastic idea which you then write up into an impressive proposal and then pitch as if your life (or career) depended on it, you may be successful. If you're very, very lucky!

Before we start, it's good to know the fundamentals. Broadcasters (the companies that transmit programmes) are either producer broadcasters like the BBC and ITV (making some of their own programmes) or they're publisher broadcasters like Channel 4 and Five (buying in all their programmes). Either way, for a production company to get their programme on screen, they generally need to sell their idea to a broadcaster who will then commit to financing some or all of it. The people at the broadcasters who do this are called commissioning editors.

Having good meetings with commissioners is key to getting your ideas on-screen. *Who Wants To Be A Millionaire?* was commissioned only because the production company encouraged the commissioning editor to play the game for himself (with £1000 rather than a million), and he was hooked.

You can get to know commissioning editors in several ways. You can try emailing them direct asking for a meeting, but this is unlikely to succeed if you haven't made something for them already. Alternatively, you can attend a PACT open day where commissioners are present (PACT is the producers' trade association). Or you can go to the right dinner parties!

The process of developing a programme and getting it commissioned is as follows:

Step 1: generating the idea
Step 2: writing the proposal
Step 3: pitching it to a commissioning editor
Step 4: celebrating the commission with alcohol (step 4 is rare!)

Let's go through these one at a time.

Step 1: generating the idea

This is harder than it sounds, especially if you're less of a development team and more of a development one-man band. Looking at a blank piece of paper and coming up with a hit concept is practically impossible. This is why most companies employ more than one development researcher, so that people can bounce ideas off each other. Creative sparks have more chance of becoming raging infernos if someone else fans the flames. (That may be overstating it – but development is all about overstating **everything**!)

GENERATING IDEAS: 15 TOP TIPS

1. **Spend a lot of time reading newspapers and magazines**
    They're a good source of stories. They also show you what subjects people are interested in at any given time.

2. **Watch out for new books being published**
    Is there any new research being published that may be programme-worthy? Science and medicine are often fruitful areas.

3. **Keep a close eye on the calendar**
    Are any anniversaries coming up which could serve as a 'peg' for a programme? The beginning of the Second World War? The end of the Second World War? The middle of the Second World War? Forget the last one – it doesn't work. (You see, this is why you need someone else in the room when you're generating ideas: 'Middle of the Second World War? Are you mad? There's no specific anniversary! Where's the peg, idiot? Fancy a cuppa?')

4. **Know who is commissioning at any given time**
    Take note of who is commissioning what and which commissioner has joined which channel. Certain commissioners have likes and dislikes – and it pays to know them. There are also 'commissioning rounds' when they are actively looking for ideas.

5. **Remember that different channels have different needs at different times**
    You don't pitch the same ideas to Sky One and BBC Two – they're totally different channels. And channels have different needs at different times of the day. What they broadcast in the daytime is very different to what they put out last thing at night.

6. **Rigorously research the channels you're hoping to sell your ideas to**
    In development you have to watch lots of TV to see what is going on in the industry. Watch the channel you're about to pitch to and visit its website.

7. **Read the trade papers, such as *Broadcast***
    This will help you to be on top of each channel's ratings successes and failures. Broadcasters will not want to commission another reality show if the last three have bombed. The trade papers will also let you know if another company has just had an idea green lit which is remarkably similar to one of your own. (At that point, you find a cat and kick it.)

8. **Network with the head honchos!**
    Commissioning editors often have get-togethers where they talk about where their department is heading. It's a good idea to get to those, so that you can see which way the

programme wind is blowing. It is also a valuable opportunity to try to get some face time with the commissioner, so that they get to know what a lovely person you are.

9. Be knowledgeable about new talent
It helps if you know who's 'hot with the kids'. You may discover a star!

10. And be knowledgeable about established talent
If you or your company has a good relationship with a household name (a 'national treasure', to use a present industry buzzword), you're well on the way to getting a commission. All you need is a half decent vehicle for them. Some people say that there are only seven basic stories in the whole world. There are probably fewer fundamental programme ideas, one of which is the travelogue. If you go to a broadcaster with Stephen Fry, Griff Rhys Jones or Joanna Lumley, the word 'travelogue' and a good twist, you'll probably get a green light. If you go with a former Big Brother contestant you probably won't – no matter how good the idea.

11. Don't be tempted to copy ideas
You may draw on inspiration from elsewhere, but straight copying will be spotted a mile off. You'll never work in this industry again!

12. Keep an eye on the trends
Formats have been the rage for some time because they can be sold abroad, generating big money. A format is a programme where roughly the same thing happens in each show, but the people and locations change. Come up with a good format and you'll be drinking fine wines for the rest of your life.

13. Be sensible
Don't spend too much time thinking up one-hour standalone documentaries. They cost too much to make. With long series you get economies of scale. You can pay for one title sequence and use it many times. You can commission music and reuse it programme after programme. And hopefully you will build up a loyal viewer base. That's why commissioners prefer series.

14. Remember the basics of storytelling
Your idea must have a narrative arc: a beginning, a middle and an end. Even a programme about a complex science subject needs to progress to a conclusion at the end. It also helps if there is jeopardy, real human emotion and a compelling narrative, so that viewers want to stay with the programme.

15. You need to be able to generate dozens of great ideas from scratch
This is the hard bit. Take a deep breath and gird your loins: you're about to come up with a programme idea which could make you a millionaire. (Or maybe not. Let's see!)

GENERATING IDEAS FROM SCRATCH

One way to think up brand new ideas is to go through books of idioms or lists of song titles to see what sparks they generate in your subconscious. What programme could have that title? A simple phrase can lead to a concept that may lead to a hit show. Programmes are often all about the title, so this does make sense. Word on the TV street is that this is how *Through The Keyhole* came about. That extremely successful programme format was dreamed up by a prestigious documentary maker. It made him a lot of money – and quite right too! Below are some idioms which might generate your *Through The Keyhole* moment:

What programmes can you think of which might have the titles listed below? Do them one at a time. Write down the idiom on a piece of paper, then brainstorm some ideas for programmes. If you do this with a friend it will be easier, and more fun.

1. Small Is Beautiful
2. Bring It On!
3. Winner Takes All
4. Expiry Date
5. Fallen Angel.

Here are a few thoughts that occur to me.

Small Is Beautiful

- Filming people of restricted growth who enter beauty pageants
- A *Blind Date* type show for people under five foot
- Following a topless achondroplasic model trying to get onto Page 3.

Bring It On!

- A Saturday night challenge-based game show.

A proctologist once told me that there's more variation in anuses than in faces. He reckoned that he could name all his patients just from pictures of their anuses. On this challenge-based show, I would take this one stage further. I would get a hundred of his patients to come to the studio and bend over while wearing nothing except paper bags on their heads. He'd have to name them all in one minute. Each time he got a name right, that patient would take off their bag. What do you reckon? Bring it on!

Winner Takes All

- A high-stakes quiz show where the winner wins and the loser really loses.

I've always wanted to see a quiz show where neighbours compete for the contents of each other's houses. In this show there would be a series of general knowledge rounds so viewers can play along at home. First up – the lounge round. The neighbour who gets the most correct answers in the lounge round wins all the contents of the other neighbour's lounge. The losing neighbour is forced to watch live footage on a big screen of his consumer durables being moved from his house to his neighbour's. The look on the faces of the losing neighbour's kids as their beloved plasma TV is taken away forever! Priceless! Now, you may say that this is going a bit too far – and you're probably right – but the concept might lead to something. A development team could discuss it for a while and see if a more feasible idea emerged.

Expiry Date

- Students compete to see who can find and eat the most out-of-date food – pretty gross, but it has its attractions
- We predict people's estimated date of death by looking at their lifestyles – we then work with them to improve their predicted expiry date
- A dating show for old people – They think they're past their romance expiry date. We prove to them that they're not!

Fallen Angel

- Nurses who have fallen on hard times and have resorted to lapdancing – I'd watch that!
- Nurses who have fallen on hard times and have resorted to stripping – I'd watch that too!
- Nurses who have fallen on hard times and are now high-class escorts – you may see a theme developing!

Obviously you can get male nurses as well as female nurses – but for health and safety reasons I wouldn't recommend they slide down too many poles in the nude.

So, we've generated some ideas. I'm sure yours are better than mine. But how can you tell if your idea is a winner?

1. A good idea is usually very simple and can be summed up in no more than two lines. If it takes ages for you to explain your idea, then it's probably rubbish.
2. A good idea needs to be affordable. There is no point in having an expensive idea like spending six months sailing with a Hollywood star down the Amazon and pitching it to a minor channel that is poor and couldn't possibly afford to commission it.
3. A good idea needs WDITOT (or 'widdytot', as I call it: ie, 'Why Didn't I Think Of That?'). The best ideas seem obvious – after someone else has had them.

If you have an idea that you think has potential, the next stage is to write up a proposal. This is a document outlining the idea which you'll send to broadcasters. The proposal writing stage can take up months of your life and reduce you to a gibbering wreck, but it's unavoidable. I once tried getting out of writing a proposal on a subject I knew nothing about. It so annoyed my boss at the time that she said my career was in the toilet and she was about to flush the chain. Now that would be a good game show!

Every company has their own house style. Some like a proposal to be on one page. Others like more detail and lots of pages. Here's a house style from the latter category.

FRONT PAGE CONTENTS

Your company logo at the top

Do anything you can to reinforce the point that this is your company's idea, and you would prefer that someone else didn't steal it. This has been known to happen and causes understandable consternation in the company which had the original idea.

The proposed programme title

The title of your programme is extremely important. Viewers should know what the programme is just from the title. It needs to be 'what it says on the tin'. *Basket Weaving in Peru* is clearly not a shiny floor, studio-based game show, but at least you can tell what it is from the title.

The subtitle

Below the title a subtitle is generally a good idea to flesh out the idea a little bit.

The offering

The offering is the duration of the programmes: how many you'd like to make and for which channel.

The pictures

It's a good idea to have some striking pictures on the front page. The front page has to grab their attention. Images are a great way to do it.

The sell

The front page should feature a punchy paragraph that really sells the programme idea. Really sells it. Sells it better than you've ever sold anything in your life before. Not just your life. Your entire family's lives. See where I'm going with this? This paragraph needs to have lots of sexy TV words. 'Exclusive access', 'Never seen before footage', 'Gripping personal stories', etc.

Less is not more when it comes to proposal writing. In fact 'more' isn't usually enough. It needs to be much 'more'. Think 'more', squared.

Obviously, this is the place where you make sure the commissioner is aware that you have a 'national treasure' presenter on board. If you haven't, just pray your paragraph is so sexy that they don't notice (they will). There are degrees of sexiness, though. You will 'sex up' a proposal more for Sky than you would for BBC Four or Channel 4. They are likely to prefer an intelligent, sexy approach (think Carol Vorderman in her early Countdown days).

PAGE 1 CONTENTS

Suggested slot and reason
It might be an idea for the reader to get their breath back after all the sexiness of the front page. So at the top of page 1, include a paragraph spelling out your suggested slot for the programme and statistical proof why it would work in that slot. Stick some really persuasive viewer data in there.

The format
It's time to outline exactly what the show is about and what the first programme would contain. You still need to have words that are full of energy and passion, but now you're getting down to the nuts and bolts of the programme itself. This will take up the rest of the page, because there's so much great content to talk about, isn't there?

PAGE 2 CONTENTS

This is where you can start to go a bit 'off piste', depending on the genre of programme. If it's about an elite police squad, then page 2 could include some 'FMFs' (er, how can I put this – 'Make Love To Me Facts').

- How many arrests do they make 'every single day'?
- How many seriously violent drug dealers, rapists and murderers have they slammed behind bars in the last year alone?
- How many of their brave officers have been injured carrying out their life-endangering duties in the recent past? (Note: How you define 'recent past' is up to you – a lot of statistic-bending goes on in proposals!)

You may have room on page 2 for your main characters and their photos as well. A good TV show needs characters that viewers care about – it's important that they either love them or hate them. Ambivalence is not an option. So you should include pen portraits of your main contributors. Don't be afraid to resort to the old Hollywood clichés: 'veteran cops', 'rookies keen to make an impression', 'chalk and cheese partners', etc.

PAGE 3 CONTENTS

Establish that there will be no shortage of content
Page 3 could establish that you would definitely have enough material for a long series. Go into all the stories that you could have got with these coppers if you'd been filming them for a couple of months last summer.

Sketch out the series

How would it develop? I would suggest that the stories resolve in each programme rather than going for a serial soap opera approach. Would the programmes be themed? Perhaps raise this as an option for the commissioner to consider. Make them feel in charge!

Biographies

Page 3 may be the place for a biography of your on-screen talent, if it's a presenter-led show. If they aren't sufficiently well known, you need to illustrate why they are ideal for this programme. If they are a household name, perhaps a line or two about why they're passionate about this subject. You may need to establish that they won't just 'phone in' their performance. 'X [insert presenter's name] has always been interested in lesser spotted skinks and how their habitat is shrinking.'

PAGE 4 CONTENTS

The 'look' of the programme

This could be where you discuss the 'look' of the programme. Will it have drama reconstructions with Hollywood production values? What about CGI? Specially composed music? This is a chance to sell the technical side of your show.

Off-screen talent

You may even go into the off-screen talent. Have you secured the services of a director who has just come off a hit series? If so, make sure you mention it.

Proposed schedule

This page could include your proposed schedule for making the programme. Remember that the commissioning editor wants high-quality shows with great viewing figures, delivered on time and on budget. You need to reassure them on all these points in your proposal. If they know you and you've delivered in the past, you have a much better chance of convincing them of your reliability.

PAGE 5 CONTENTS

One possible filler for page 5 and beyond is a super-detailed breakdown of a programme, rather like a shooting script with hypothetical stories, commentary, reconstructions, etc. Normally you would only go to this trouble if you've had a positive steer from a commissioner that you are in with a good chance. In fact, some broadcasters actually go to a company with an idea and say, 'We're interested in this, can you have a look at it and come up with a proposal?' If this happens, or you get development money from a broadcaster to progress an idea, you're in good shape.

So you've had your idea, and you've written it up into a proposal. Now comes the fun bit!

A PERSONAL VIEW

Pitching isn't easy. Some people are good at it. Some people are pants. The latter generally hate doing it and avoid it like the plague. The former quite like the masochistic nature of the pitching process. You're putting your ideas and creative 'babies' on the line, just waiting for them to be picked apart and then slaughtered by a ruthless commissioner.

When pitching you need to remember Direct TV Training's 'golden rule': look at it from the other person's point of view. The commissioner is under enormous pressure to deliver ratings. If he fails to do that he may be fired, in a very public and embarrassing way. If your idea isn't right for their channel, or is fundamentally flawed, or if you're exaggerating what is achievable, then you can expect to be shown the door (and quite right too). However, if your idea is the next *Millionaire* or *Weakest Link*, then the world is your oyster (and your bank manager is about to become your best friend!)

Whether you like pitching or not, we are in the ideas business. Inevitably, you will be pitching ideas at some level. It may not be to the Head of Programmes at Channel 4, but every time you're selling a story to your producer, or suggesting a contributor to the series editor, or proposing a money-saving wheeze to the production manager, you're pitching!

Below there are some tips on pitching to commissioning editors. Everyone has their own style when it comes to pitching meetings. Some people think a gimmick can make their pitch more memorable. If their show is a docusoap about a farm they'll take a pig in with them, that kind of thing. So feel free to put your own spin on my suggestions.

PITCHING: 10 TOP TIPS

1. **Preparation is crucial**
   Before the pitching meeting with the commissioner, prepare yourself for the areas you will be expected to address. You will need to establish what time slot you think your proposed programme should go into, why it's perfect for that slot, what is new about your idea and why it's an ideal fit for their channel. Don't go in to see the broadcaster without all these things already clear in your mind.

2. **Gear your pitch to the specific commissioner**
   You might take your fantastic idea to a number of commissioning editors to see if they bite. Change your pitch each time according to the particular vibe of their channel and the commissioner's personal preferences. Some commissioners like loads of detail; others like to talk in a more esoteric way: 'What's the *essence* of the programme?' The latter species is increasingly rare. Nowadays it's a lot more pragmatic – 'bums on seats' and all that.

3. **Rehearse it before you go in**

Try to predict their questions and mentally rehearse your answers to them. Memorise key facts and helpful statistics. It might even be worth role playing your pitch with colleagues. Ask them to grill you and give you a hard time. This could help you spot any flaws in your idea.

4. **Start with a firm handshake**

Don't go in there all sheepish and shy – TV isn't a place for timidity. A commissioner might chew you up and spit you out if you show a sign of weakness – some are nice, but some aren't. They are under a lot of pressure, after all.

5. **Don't oversell too much**

You have to 'spin' your idea so it sounds great, but if you oversell it too much you'll be found out. Most commissioners have made programmes themselves and know what is possible and what isn't. If you promise the moon on a stick, and the commissioner is well aware that the budget won't run to a stick and the moon has just signed up to a rival broadcaster, you'll be shown the door quickly. Even if this isn't spotted at this stage, you can be sure that it will be at the first viewing of your moonless, stickless programme. You and your company will never get a commission out of them again.

6. **Expect a cross-examination**

A lot of money is on the line, so the meeting probably won't be like a friendly chat down the pub. You should expect tough questions. Try to build up a head of steam early on: pitch your idea confidently, then brace yourself for their response. Answer any questions politely and with assurance. If you don't know the answer, say so. Making it up as you go along is not a good idea. 'So I'm led to believe' is the worst thing you can possibly say.

7. **Get them to think it's their idea**

The sooner you can get the commissioner to buy into the idea and start making suggestions, the better. If they feel part of the creative process, they're more likely to commission your programme. They will like the collegiate feel of the meeting – it's brainstorming like they used to do when they first started out. If they enjoy your pitch, it's more likely they'll agree to further meetings with you in the future.

8. **Agree with whatever they say**

If they do make a suggestion, agree with it. You may be wedded to doing your programme in a studio, but if they want it at various exterior locations, run with their idea. The customer is always right.

9. **Remember: if your idea's a winner, it's great for them too**

If your programme is a cracker, the commissioner has as much to gain from its success as you. This should give you confidence. The commissioner who can say he green lit *Deal Or No Deal* must have dined out on it for years. I mean, how does that programme work? I don't know – but it does.

10. Leave on a good note

Always leave with a cheery smile, even if you've crashed and burned. It will stand you in good stead for next time. Most commissioners will want a few meetings with you before they green light anything. They like to get the full measure of you and your company before committing. Play it long!

So, what happens if they love your idea? Each broadcaster will have different rules. Some aim to respond within a week, others can take six months. Occasionally they give you money to develop the idea further. They may even give you enough to make a pilot version of the programme to see if it works. More often they will say, 'Thanks, but no thanks!' However, sometimes – very rarely – you do get a green light. A precious commission! If this happens go straight to step 4!

Step 4: celebrating the commission!

With alcohol - and lots of it! In the event of a commission, even the rule about not throwing up in front of your boss goes out of the window. (As does your vomit, if you time it right.)

After the celebratory party there will be lots of negotiating with the channel about talent, money and production staff. The budget is always smaller and the schedule always tighter than you would like, but you somehow find a way to work with what you've got.

Then, finally, your company gets to make the programme, and you might even get the chance to work on it after all your hard work getting it commissioned – if you're very lucky!

Chapter 8:
Producer/Director Tips

Chapter 8: Producer/Director Tips

I've series produced dozens of shows for various broadcasters, including ITV, Channel 4, Five, Discovery US, National Geographic, Animal Planet and Sky. I've also produced and directed hundreds of programmes in a wide variety of genres, including factual entertainment, wildlife, documentary, history, talk, medical, police, corporate, sport and current affairs. I'm still learning all the time, and still making silly mistakes from time to time.

Quite a few directors who are 30 years or more into their career will come out with statements such as: 'I think I'm getting the hang of this now!' How many other jobs are like that? I bet lawyers, accountants and surgeons think they've got the hang of their jobs pretty early on – well, let's hope surgeons do. But that's one of the great things about TV. It keeps you constantly on your toes.

All this is a roundabout way of saying that, even if you're a highly experienced producer/director, it's worth you reading this chapter. You may well disagree with my suggestions, but at least it will get you questioning the best ways to do things. And if you're a rookie producer/director, it is well worth absorbing this stuff, if only so that you can reject it and do it your own way, once you have more experience.

As a producer/director it's likely that you will have worked your way up through the ranks – runner, researcher, associate producer, etc – so you'll have mastered those skills. But being a producer/director involves being on top of all that and so much more. I have a reputation for being an uber-organised producer/director. Perhaps too meticulous at times, so bear that in mind if you prefer a more laid-back 'see how it goes approach'. However, with tight schedules being the current norm, there's a limit to how much you can 'busk' it these days.

If you have a clear plan and a clear idea what you need, I think it's easier to go 'off piste' if things do change – but like skinning a cat, there are many ways to make a TV programme.

In this chapter you'll find my take on various elements of being a producer/director. First, some thoughts on what you can do before your shoot to help it go more smoothly. There are tips on writing good shooting scripts and how to make the most out of a recce – where you check out the location, contributors and logistics in advance.

For advice on how to make the most out of the shoot itself, I suggest you refer to Chapter 6 on the shooting associate producer role, in particular the producing and directing sections.

Most of the principles are the same, the only major difference is that now you are shooting with a crew. You need to communicate clearly to the cameraman and sound recordist what you want and listen to their suggestions. The best advice I was given about working with crews is to remember to give them tea breaks. It is important and easily overlooked.

As a producer/director you're also more likely to be handling on-screen talent. For tips on this go to Chapter 9 and apply the 'golden rule': put yourself in the presenter's shoes. Being a presenter is tough, and they are hugely reliant on their producer/directors to make it easier for them. You and your presenter are a team – you need to work together. Try to gauge early on whether they want to make suggestions and contribute to the script or just be told what to do. Accommodate their wishes and be polite at all times (except when the light is dropping and the local pubs are about to close!).

At the end of this chapter you'll find suggestions on preparing for a foreign shoot and some thoughts on post-production and commentary.

Before your shoot

PRODUCING SHOOTING SCRIPTS

It's crucial to prepare some sort of shooting script in advance of filming. Over the page is my personal template, which I've found extremely helpful in organising my thoughts before I go out and direct. It has a column down the left-hand side which maps out the sound content in the order of the final edited film (ie the producer bits), and on the right-hand side a column which outlines the pictures to go with that sound content (ie the director bits).

After the shoot you need to adjust your original shooting script to reflect more accurately what actually happened on location. It never goes totally to plan! Then you should view your rushes and put timecodes into the handy columns in the middle of the template. This makes your shooting script into an edit script. You can leave this edit script with the editor while you put your feet up and relax. Or more likely go and film something else.

Before the shoot you may want to show your shooting script to the cameraman. You should certainly discuss it with your researcher, who should have creative suggestions of his own. Plus he'll have talked to the contributors and will have good ideas for questions – and thoughts on areas to avoid!

SHOOTING SCRIPT

Sound	Sound timecodes	Picture timecodes	Pictures
In this column write in the sound content you expect to hear in your final piece. This includes rough commentary and bullet points of the content you want from your actuality sequences and interviews.	Fill in sound timecodes by reviewing tapes after shoot.	Fill in picture timecodes by reviewing tapes after shoot.	In this column write descriptions of the picture sequences you need to film to go with the contents of the sound column.
eg, **COMM** Family liaison officer John Smith has one of the toughest jobs in the police service. He helps victim's families.			eg, shots of John getting out of police car and leaving frame.
JOHN IV • Why do you do your job? • Is it hard not to take it home with you? • How does it impact on your own family?			• John walking to park with his kids. • Playing with kids on swings. • Intercut with sync sound of interview – shot CU. Eyeline close to camera. Looking R to L.
COMM John's mother worked in a bank. She was killed by an armed robber in 2002. John joined the police force three months later.			JPEG of John's mum. Slow zoom in.
JOHN IV • Tell me about what happened to your mum • How did her death affect you? • What role did it play in you joining the police service?			• John looking at newspaper cuttings about the case. • John watching home movies of his mum. • Intercut with sync IV for emotional bits. BCU where appropriate. No zooms during answers.

One of the beauties of this template is that it helps you remember to get shots to go with the commentary. Another is that when it becomes an edit script, you can see quickly if you've got too much content to fit into your final piece, or too little. If there's too much, chop bits out of your paper edit. It's quicker doing it on paper than in the edit suite. If you've got too little, you need to go out and film some more!

Hopefully I've convinced you about the usefulness of shooting scripts. Next, the value of a productive recce.

How to have a productive recce

A PERSONAL VIEW

We've all done it: set up a shoot with a cast of thousands, then turned up to find the location totally unsatisfactory. It's the worst feeling in the world. You stand there shuffling your feet, looking at the ground, or (more sensibly) get on the phone to try to solve the problem – sometimes to no avail.

On an ITV show I series produced we rolled up one evening to a scrapyard to film some sequences with an expert. We were half an hour late and it was all locked up. Everyone had gone home. We tried doing some filming outside the scrapyard. A nearby fish processing plant agreed to lend us some electricity, but our lights kept tripping their fuses. We had to abandon the shoot. It was a nightmare, and very embarrassing.

The moral of the story? Get your researcher to phone your next location if you're going to be late. You will know that you're falling behind schedule before anyone else, so let your researcher know, and always make sure that he has the phone numbers of the people with the keys! That is part of a producer/director's job, reminding researchers what they need to have covered. Some researchers are inexperienced, and most are overworked. You need to help them remember things in the nicest possible way.

On another shoot in India we were filming an experiment to see if cobras could hear airborne sounds. We needed to find an isolated location which was totally silent for the experiment to have any validity. When we arrived at the place that the associate producer had found, it was next to a busy road! (In his defence, he had only just recovered from typhoid.) We found a fall-back option in the countryside, but as soon as we started filming the snake, a local cement factory started up the pile driver. We couldn't believe it. Our rigorous experiment didn't work out, and we had to play the sequence for laughs instead.

I'll never know for sure, but I do think that if I had personally recced these locations, things would have turned out differently. Meeting and charming the owner of the scrapyard would have reduced the chances of him going home before we turned up. I had a clear idea of the conditions I wanted for the snake experiment, and consequently would have heard the sound issues and found a better alternative. The problem was that the schedules were too tight for producer/director recces to happen – and when that's the case, things often do go wrong.

Reasons for recceing

The real shame is that increasingly, recces are seen as an expendable luxury. They are not. A good recce will help a producer/director to:

- Spot technical and logistical problems
- Find potentially good people and locations
- Schedule the shoot effectively
- Sort out any financial issues before the crew and talent turn up.

Recces are the ideal opportunity to apply Direct TV Training's 'golden rule': imagine you're each member of the crew and look at the location and contributors from their perspective. This will lead to a productive recce and increase your chances of a successful shoot. Let's do it one by one.

On a recce . . .

1. IMAGINE YOU'RE THE PRODUCTION MANAGER

You don't want any unpleasant financial surprises on the shoot. Often, it's best to discuss facility fees face-to-face in advance of filming. The recce is also a chance to check out financial minutiae. Will you be charged for power for lights, battery charging, etc? It's better to know now. If they want cash on the day and you don't have any, valuable time could be wasted going to the cashpoint!

However, before you do any negotiating, you should check what your budget is and that you're authorised to do deals. Some production managers worry that 'creatives' are inclined to throw money at things in order to get their pretty shots. My tip is to treat your budget as if it is your own money. If the production manager sees you being careful with the cash, they're more likely to put a good word in for you next time a producer/director job comes up!

2. IMAGINE YOU'RE THE PRODUCTION COORDINATOR

What will make filming easier? For example, it's always useful to have a base at the location. Somewhere you can sit and have a cuppa, leave kit, do the presenter's make-up, etc. On the recce, find somewhere suitable and negotiate access and a fee. You can also check that crew and contributor parking is going to be okay.

3. IMAGINE YOU'RE THE ELECTRICIAN

Where are the power points and what are they like? Recently I was looking for an old house for a drama reconstruction and found what seemed ideal, until we saw that the sockets were prehistoric. They were likely to have blown up if we tried to plug TV lights into them. We established that we couldn't afford a generator on our budget and found somewhere else. Without a recce we'd have been knackered.

4. IMAGINE YOU'RE THE DIRECTOR OF PHOTOGRAPHY

Investigate lighting issues. Assess whether the windows and natural light will be a help or a hindrance. Sun shining through a window will affect the amount of lighting needed and may cause continuity problems. Venetian blinds in the back of a shot can create a nasty flickering effect. Do you need to put neutral density filters on all the windows so you have more control over the lighting? It's better to decide now than on the day.

5. IMAGINE YOU'RE THE RESEARCHER

What grief could come the researcher's way on the shoot? If you're filming in an office you can minimise potential issues by making sure that everyone knows about the upcoming filming. Charm the workers that are there, and put up a notice about the impending shoot for the ones that aren't. Then, if the researcher gets hassle during filming, he can say: 'Sorry, we thought you knew about it. We put posters up/sent round an email/told you about it two weeks ago when we visited.'

It's also wise to be honest about how long filming will take. You don't want them shutting up shop when you have another five sequences to film. It's better to negotiate the extra £20 for the caretaker to work late now rather than on the day.

You should also try to find more potential contributors on the recce. Imagine you're the researcher and someone drops out last minute. It helps to have reserves, and the recce is an ideal time to find them.

6. IMAGINE YOU'RE THE SOUND RECORDIST

What sound issues are going to make your life difficult? If there is noisy air conditioning, can it be switched off on the day? If there are roadworks nearby, will they still be there when you're filming? Are you on a flight path? Is there a school within earshot? If so, you had better avoid filming during the lunchbreak.

If there is background music, can it be turned off? If it can't, you had better find somewhere else to film, otherwise you won't be able to edit your sequence. It's wise to schedule the recce for the same time of day that you're likely to be shooting: this will give you a better idea of potential sound issues.

7. IMAGINE YOU'RE THE HEALTH AND SAFETY OFFICER

The recce is a chance to look for hazards that will help you fill in the risk assessment form. In addition, you can check access to the location. The crew won't like it if they have to lug heavy equipment up 20 flights of stairs because the lift is out of order. Check that there are viable routes to and from your location.

8. IMAGINE YOU'RE THE COMPANY LAWYER

Always turn up for filming with permissions in writing – preferably from the right person! The recce is a good chance to finalise paperwork.

9. PUT YOUR 'DIRECTOR'S HAT' ON

The recce is a great chance to start thinking about visuals. Look out for nice shots and potential 'banana skins'. I almost ended up doing a shoot for *Mr Right* (an ITV show presented by Ulrika Jonsson) in a restaurant where an entire wall was covered in mirrors. It would have been impossible to light and shoot. Thank goodness for the recce.

10. PUT YOUR 'PRODUCER'S HAT' ON

Start warming up the contributors. You can get to know them better and reassure them about the filming, perhaps rehearse a few interview topics to see how articulate they are. Also, you can get a feel for whether they are likely to drop out. If they are wobbly, you need to start the process of keeping them on board. (For tips on what you can say, go to 'Keeping contributors on board' in Chapter 5 on page 64 onwards.)

11. IMAGINE YOU'RE MARCO POLO!

Get a local map. Maps are very handy for spotting problems and opportunities. You can look for sources of noise such as airports, motorways or schools. Also, you can look for top shot options. Is there a block of flats nearby? You might be able to negotiate access to the roof – it is easier to do this in advance than on the day. And you can add the map and order of locations to the call sheet, so that people can find their way around more easily on the shoot.

A good recce will help your filming go super-smoothly, but there are some shoots where a recce isn't usually feasible, and that is filming abroad. The stakes are high with foreign shoots (budgets are higher, schedules tighter) so you need to achieve everything that you would on a recce over the phone. Language difficulties and time differences can complicate matters, but it's all worth it in the end. Check out the suntan!

Foreign filming: what you need to know

A PERSONAL VIEW

I've been lucky enough to film all over the world. It's an experience, that's for sure. Not always a happy experience, but it's certainly intense, and that is what life is all about – highs and lows. Here is a good example.

As I briefly mentioned earlier, one documentary I've worked on involved me posing undercover as a paedophile in the Far East for a couple of months. We were trying to get the British law changed so that sex tourists could be prosecuted back in Britain if they had sex with children abroad. Other countries had this law. Britain didn't.

The way we were going to achieve this was filming British sex tourists picking up children, and the best way to do this was by posing as paedophiles with hidden cameras and microphones. The hidden camera was a lens in the badge of my fisherman's jacket-type waistcoat, and the microphone looked like a pen sticking out of the pocket.

Two problems here: one was that the fisherman's jacket style was what journalists wore in that neck of the woods. The other was that the camera would make a small clicking noise when the tape ran out. This could be audible to the pimp menacing you or the prostitute sat on your lap.

When I arrived, I found out that the last journalist who had tried to expose sex tourism in that area of the country had had his head cut off – by the local mayor. (Even Boris Johnson wouldn't have done that.)

Undeterred, I started going to the local brothels, asking for children for sex (purely for research purposes), and one American sex bar owner was very aloof. I wanted to expose this guy – he was a real sleazebag – but he wouldn't talk to me for days on end. Eventually he walked into the next-door brothel, saw me chatting to a prostitute and apologised for being rude.

He said that he had seen my newly-grown beard (that was a mistake) and thought I was FBI. He whispered, 'You were asking all those questions, and the FBI have been trying to catch me for years.' Without further ado, he invited me back to his place and began to spill the beans on (hidden) camera: how he had smuggled cocaine into Canada in car tyres and BMW parts into the Philippines – with the help of two passports, obviously. He was on top form; then he announced that no one crossed him because he had 'friends' in the local army, police force and local government. 'I can get someone killed in half an hour,' he said. I can't run very far in half an hour. I only have short legs.

Shortly after that, one of his prostitutes asked to borrow my 'pen'. If she had got hold of the microphone, all the wires would have come out and I would have been a dead man. I was very lucky I had a spare pen.

When I returned to Britain I went to see my dentist because I had bad toothache. Apparently, I had been grinding my teeth in my sleep while I was away because I was under such stress. Even when I got back to the hotel at night I couldn't let anyone know that I was really an investigative TV journalist, not a paedophile. Word would have got round, and it would have been Goodnight Vienna.

That shoot was quite an experience. At times it was horrendous. When my dear friend and colleague Tim Tate arrived I said, 'Welcome to Hell' and meant it. But we did get the programme made and we did get the law changed, and most importantly, I got another anecdote for the collection.

It is always important to prepare properly for a shoot, but this is especially the case for foreign filming. If something goes wrong when you're filming abroad the consequences can be horrendous. Here are some tips on what you can do before you go to reduce the possibility of this happening.

Preparing for filming abroad

PRODUCER/DIRECTOR TIPS: BEFORE YOU FLY

1. **Pick a good team**
    If you're going to be stuck in a jungle with these guys for weeks on end, it really helps if you like each other. At least to begin with.

2. **Pick them early**
    You should select the crew earlier than usual. This gives them more time to sort out their lives and your team more time to get their visas. Pester your production manager to get

the crew to sign and send their contracts. It is not just contributors who can drop out on you at the last minute.

3. **Check insurance**

   Make sure that you are covered for everything. A few years back I was hired for a wildlife shoot abroad, and on the way to the airport the production company told me that I wasn't insured. They asked me to sign a document that signed my life away – if I was eaten during filming, 'it had nothing to do with them'. Charming. About five days later I was being chased up a tree by a rhino!

4. **Clarify the money arrangements on your shoot**

   Is everyone on daily allowances (also known as 'Per Diems') or 'actuality' expenses? Per diems are a fixed daily amount, so it's down to you to fund your lunch and dinner. 'Actuality' is where you get a float of petty cash, pay for meals, keep receipts and justify it when you get back. Ideally, your researcher will handle this on a day-to-day basis, but you are responsible overall for the finances – so keep on top of it.

5. **Pack early**

   If you're filming abroad, you have a lot to think about. I suggest packing as early as you can during the week before you go: it gives you more chance to remember what you may have forgotten. This applies to your personal kit and the crew equipment for the shoot. It's no good getting to the airport and noticing that the camera is the wrong specification!

6. **Be realistic about timescales**

   Assume that everything will take much longer than it would in Britain. This will help you devise a realistic schedule.

7. **Check the weather forecast**

   Try not to fly out in monsoon season or the hottest time of year, but if this is unavoidable, make sure that everyone takes the right clothes and equipment. In the good old days the production company would pay for a shopping spree to kit you up. In fact, I'm still wearing my monsoon-proof 'paedophile' shoes right now – 15 years later. They don't make them like that anymore!

8. **Choose local fixers with care**

   Foreign fixers are absolutely essential and excellent value for money. I've only ever had one bad one (he was ripping us off left, right and centre). They help you get around, communicate with locals and get the best deals. Don't let your production manager try to save money by slashing the fixer from the budget.

9. **Beware local crews**

   If you can afford to fly British crews out for the shoot, then do so. Local crews can be very unpredictable, and they don't have the same TV background as us Brits. An internal cutaway to us may not be an internal cutaway to them. They may think all general views (GVs) should be mute, even if a lorry drives straight through shot. If you do need to use local crews, try to get out there early and arrange to meet as many potential crews as you can. The more options the better!

10. Brief the crew well

Make sure you speak to your crew over the phone and fully brief them on the shoot. Send them your shooting script. Make sure the production manager calls them and checks that they have all their documents. Get the researcher to phone them and introduce themselves. When you go away the researcher is often the bridge between the crew and the busy, stressed-out director. This is an important relationship – make sure the researcher knows that.

11. Arrange local currency

How much do you need to get? When should you order it? What is best, travellers cheques or cash? The money side of things is such a headache. If you need to bribe someone to get access to an important location, you will need lots of cash – they won't take a credit card! Delegate this to your researcher on the proviso that they guarantee 100% that you'll never be short of beer tokens. (After all, you do need alcohol to fuel your creative muse!)

12. Take your time over the risk assessment form

The risk assessment form isn't fun to do, but it does need doing properly. It could save your life – or your career, if something happens on location and you are taken to court.

I did a series called *Stunt School* in Australia. It was about stunt rookies learning the tricks of the danger trade. Every day involved dangerous stunts being done by amateurs. As you can imagine, the risk assessment form was pretty sizeable, but not as big as the one for the king cobra shoot in India (which didn't stop me being bitten by a snake), or the one for the reptile shoot on Krakatoa (which didn't stop me falling off the volcano). I guess the point is that you can't predict everything, but you can predict some things, and you should certainly have plans ready if something terrible does happen.

13. Insurance and medical forms

Be sure to have these handy.

14. Take someone on the shoot with First Aid training

Have these handy too!

So, you're all prepped and ready to go – but things can still go wrong at the last minute…

ORGANISING FILM CREWS AT THE AIRPORT: THREE TOP TIPS

1. **Moving kit**

    On *O'Shea's Big Adventure* we had 50 steel boxes full of kit. It was like moving a small army around the world. We used to put red tape on one of the handles of each of our boxes: this reduced the risk of leaving something behind on the carousel. We also carefully counted the boxes on the trolleys before leaving the airport. There was only one problem with this system: counting up to 50 can be quite a challenge when you are jet lagged and/or substantially inebriated from the flight.

2. **Excess baggage allowance**

    Part of the producer/director foreign filming game is avoiding paying excess baggage fees at airports. This is obviously quite a challenge when you have 50 big cases and all your personal bags. You can try the following techniques:

    -   Charm the check-in lady
    -   Offer her signed photographs of the presenter
    -   Pretend to film the team checking in, so that the airline gets some free publicity. (If all those fail, put your foot under the scale!)

    (Incidentally, if you want your crew to pretend to film something without actually switching the camera on, ask the cameraman to use the 'strawberry filter' or film a 'Dutch take'. He will know what you mean.)

3. **Getting tapes through customs**

    This often causes a row. Customs wants to open all your tape boxes. You don't want them to. They want to put them through their old, 1970s X-ray machines. You'd really rather they didn't. This can lead to a full and frank exchange of views. (How I haven't been shot in various airports in developing countries around the world, I'll never know.)

Once through the airport you're off and running. There are other foreign filming tips in Chapter 5. Those are written primarily for researchers, but it's best if you know them all too – you might need to remind your researcher to do them!

Oh, and one final piece of advice given to me with a totally straight face by a South African game ranger during a safety briefing: 'If you come across a sedated lion in the jungle, don't put your fingers in its mouth or up its anus, because you could "activate the animal"'. Lucky I told you that, eh?

So, let's assume you've followed all my pre-shoot tips, the shoot has gone smoothly and you have got some great stuff in the can. All being well, your hard-worked team is still talking to you. They may not be. Tempers can get frayed towards the end of a long shoot, especially in the jungle. Even if your filming has degenerated into a battle of egos and a conflict of artistic differences, for the rest of your team the war is over, but not for you. The best bit is yet to come…

A PERSONAL VIEW

In my opinion, post-production (editing, dubbing, etc) is the most enjoyable part of the programme-making process. Pre-production is always stressful. Have we got enough stories? Can we shoot everything we need in this tight schedule? Who is going to drop out next? And so on. Filming is even more stressful. The light's dropping and the presenter wants to go home. It's starting to rain and the camera's broken. The crew members are hungry and they haven't had a mealbreak for hours. And so on.

However, post-production is usually great. It's like a big jigsaw puzzle. You have all the pieces and it is down to you and the editor to put them all together. Sunlight isn't an issue. The material is in the can. You don't have a big crew to manage and there are fewer things that can go wrong.

This is not to say that it's a stroll in the park. Viewings can be an ordeal akin to having all your teeth drilled at the dentist's. (Viewings are where the executives come in, watch your programme and occasionally tear it to pieces.) The odd technical issue in the edit can age you rapidly too – bad sound and a camera fault are upsetting my karma right at this moment, but editing is still the best part of the job – and it doesn't involve you getting wet.

THE 12 STAGES OF POST-PRODUCTION

1.   The assembly

This is where you bolt your footage together. You don't worry about jump cuts; it's just a case of getting all the important bits in so you can see how long it is. If you are making an hour-long programme and your assembly is five hours, you need to slash and burn before you go any further. The last thing you want is your editor spending precious time finessing material which has no chance of making the final show. I suggest you get it down to 15 minutes over, maximum. If you can 'drive' an edit suite yourself (your editor may show you how) then it is often easier to chop bits out on your own after your editor has gone home. However, it is best that you do it on a duplicate cut, in case you delete everything! After you have the assembly down to a workable length, you can move on to the next stage...

2.   The rough cut

Now it's beginning to look like a TV programme. It's only about 15 minutes over so you can start to add pictures and 'gash commentary' (rough commentary using your voice). The programme structure should be starting to make sense. Keep pruning the less important bits so that you are whittling it down towards the right duration. Now you can start asking yourself the all-important questions. Is the programme working? Have you 'set out your stall' clearly enough at the top of the programme? This is a TV term for explaining what the programme is all about. Do the narrative arcs work? Will viewers stay with it to the end? Do you have good 'teases' before the part breaks so that people will keep watching after the adverts? Does it all make sense? Well, you are about to find out, because towards the end of this stage it's time for the first viewing.

3. The first viewing

The executives and series producer come to watch your rough cut. This is always nerve-wracking, like having your homework marked at school in front of the whole class. They sit there scribbling notes. You try to gauge their reactions. Do they like it? What are they thinking? Are they going to ask for loads of work to be done to it? Why are they laughing in the wrong bits? Was that an irritated 'tut'?

My tip is, always try to get your rough cut looking as finessed as possible before the first viewing. Black holes and obvious mistakes don't breed confidence in executives. They are used to seeing completed programmes, so the more complete yours looks, the less pain you're likely to endure.

There is nothing worse than a viewing with 'blood on the cutting room floor', but painful though they may be, viewings are essential. They do make your programme better. When you have eaten, slept and breathed a project for months on end, there are times when you can't see the wood for the trees. People who know what they are talking about see your show with a fresh eye and usually make helpful suggestions. Here is another tip: if they do ask for lots of changes, treat it as an opportunity to impress them with your willingness to take their thoughts on board. Digest and respond to their input as politely as you can, then progress to the next stage.

4. The fine cut

This is the nicest part: the finessing stage. You perfect the pictures and bring the programme down to its transmission length, taking into account the execs' suggestions. You take out the 'erms' and suddenly your contributors seem extremely articulate. You improve the commentary so that it guides the viewer seamlessly through the programme, and you add music. The choice of music is crucially important. It may be especially composed for the programme if you have lots of money in the budget to pay for a composer. More likely, however, it will be library music chosen from a vast array of CDs. The music tracks need to add to the emotion of the piece – enhance the vibe, not distract from it. This can be a hard thing to pull off; everyone's music tastes differ, but it makes all the difference to your programme if you get it right. Then it's...

5. Viewing time again!

The second viewing is usually less painful than the first. The executives have seen it once, they have had their input and it's starting to look more like they envisaged in the first place. The programme now has their creative stamp, so if they rip it apart, they're really ripping themselves apart too. The executives will still make some suggestions though: they usually have issues with the commentary, and your music choices often turn out to be controversial, but the aim is to get the programme finished quick now. Everyone wants to move on with their lives – except the lawyers and compliance. This is the point where you send them a DVD and pray that there are no serious legal issues that will make your life a misery. Assuming that there aren't, you skip merrily to the next stage.

6. Picture lock

You make the final changes resulting from the second viewing and legal feedback. Graphics are added and checked: these include name captions, credits and subtitles if necessary. All this means that the programme is finished in terms of pictures, and anyone suggesting changing these do so at their peril. The cut is 'picture locked'. You might think that this is the finished programme – but you'd be wrong.

7. Dubbing

This is where you get the sound of the programme as good as it can possibly be. The sound mixer lays in all the sound tracks and mixes them together. The aim is to get the music at just the right level and the interviews as clear as a bell. Any sound effects that will help are added, and the programme now sounds immaculate (hopefully).

8. Add voiceover

The presenter or voiceover artist comes in and records the real commentary to replace your 'gash comm'. You direct them in the voiceover booth and pray that they speak at the same speed as you. If they don't, the lines won't fit into the programme! It's always strange hearing the proper voice on your programme. It feels like it is finally coming together.

9. Grading/telecine

This is where the pictures are treated so that they look as good as they possibly can. Nowadays there may not be money in the budget for grading, but when there is, you can certainly see the difference. It's amazing what a good colourist and a good machine can do.

When I was doing Stunt School I was saved by the grade. The big final day of filming in Australia was a two-camera shoot with spectacular stunts. Unfortunately, the camera assistant white balanced one camera for daylight and the other for tungsten. This meant one camera's shots were orange (like they should be in bright daylight outside), but the other camera's shots were totally blue. I needed to intercut the orange and blue shots in the programme without anyone noticing. Somehow the colourist matched them in the middle and no one knew what had gone wrong!

10. Playing out the final programme

The programme with beautiful pictures is now played out of the system onto tape and then popped down to the dubbing theatre, where the lovely sound mix is added (or vice versa – the sound mix can be played out onto the old pictures, then that tape is taken to the grade, where the nice pictures are pasted over the old pictures). Either way, your beautiful-looking and sounding baby is about to be born, but not yet. First, it has to go to quality control.

11. Quality control (QC)

A very technical person with fine attention to detail watches your programme to make sure that everything is technically correct. He checks for things that break the rules, such as flash frames or flickering images. He makes sure that the sound is acceptable. He also checks that the captions are in 'safe' – ie not on the edge of the frame so a little old lady with a black and white portable can't read every letter. After this process, your programme is officially deemed broadcastable. Next, all being well, your programme is transmitted.

12. Transmission

This is a strange sensation. Your programme somehow seems different when you watch it on the telly. You always spot things that you would like to change, but it's too late now! Sometimes the day after, you feel a bit down. All that effort, and it's suddenly all over. 'Post TX blues', they call it – but these days most programmes are repeated to death, so there is no need to feel sad!

So that's post-production – in a nutshell. I've spent quite a lot of the last two decades in edit suites. Here are some tips culled from what I've learned.

Post-production: producer/director tips

FIVE TOP TIPS IN THE EDIT

1. Be organised!

As with all TV, it is best to be organised going into the edit, which is why I've been banging on about doing an edit script. Editors like it when you go in with a written plan which you can leave them to get on with: it means that they can structure a programme quickly without you sitting there, irritating them.

2. Give the editor space

When I was younger I used to tell the editor where to make every cut. I was much too hands on; it's better to give them space so that they can weave their magic. Let them edit a part, then take a look, make some suggestions and then leave them to action those suggestions. For this to work, though, you need to follow tip number 3.

3. Choose your editor carefully

Some editors can work independently, others can't. Your programme will benefit if your editor is able to put their creative stamp on your programme and doesn't need you to call every shot.

4. Learn how to edit

Being in an edit suite with an editor is a great opportunity to learn how to edit. If you are sitting there waiting for feedback from the lawyers, use that valuable time to get some lessons – I'm sure your editor won't mind. This is an added string to your bow, and it means that next time you can do some of the 'boring' editing on an evening. If you can chop out big chunks which aren't going to make the final cut, the editor can spend more of their time making your show perfect. You could even learn to record your own 'gash comm', and lay it into the cut after your editor has gone home. This saves loads of editing time during the day.

5. **Find something productive to do during the edit**
    There can be time during the edit when the editor is doing their thing and you don't have much to do. Talking to mates on Facebook is all well and good, but your time would be better spent thinking up new programmes or writing a book! As I write this, we are playing out episodes of *Missing Mums: Lorraine Kelly Investigates* to tape. My friend and editor Simon is rather bored, but I'm having a great time writing all this helpful stuff for you! And the next incredibly helpful section is about writing commentary for factual programmes.

Writing commentary

A PERSONAL VIEW

Writing commentary is much harder than people think, but when it is done right it can make a big difference to your shows, and it can be great fun to record too. It gives us programme makers an opportunity to work with people who our mums have heard of. I've been lucky enough to use the voices of Julie Christie (*Small Miracles*), Lorraine Kelly (*Missing Mums and Missing Children*) Dennis Waterman (*Shopping from Hell*), Andrew Sachs (*Holidays from Hell*) and Lisa Rogers (*Mistresses*). I even got to fly to Los Angeles to record the voice of one of my Hollywood heroes, James Woods, for *Stunt School*.

The trick when recording famous talent is not to be intimidated. As a wise old producer once told me when I started out, even major Hollywood stars want to sound good, want direction and want more work out of you. Voiceover work is very well remunerated! So don't be shy and tell them exactly what you want (after all, actors are used to being directed every day of their working lives). However, before you get to that stage, you need to write a good script – and that's not easy.

COMMENTARY WRITING: 12 TOP TIPS

1. **What does the viewer need to know?**
    The first thing to think about when writing commentary is this: what information does the viewer need at any given point to enable them to understand what's going on? You don't

want to lose your audience when a simple explanatory line of commentary could explain to them what's happening.

2. What additional detail can you give the viewer?

As well as writing commentary to help the viewer follow your programme, you should use it to add more detail. Statistics and background can add depth to your stories, but don't overdo it – it can become distracting.

3. Spend time on your opening

The opening of your programme is often the hardest commentary section of all to write. You need to set up the story, establish a tone and sell the show hard. Take your time over it.

4. Keep it short and simple

Viewers get lost if your commentary line goes on forever, so avoid 'sub-thoughts' within the sentence. And try to use the minimum number of words. For example, when speaking, you don't normally need the word 'that': eg, 'You think that I'm writing rubbish.' Lose the word 'that' – it still makes sense.

5. Ensure that your words complement the pictures

Your commentary shouldn't describe exactly what the viewer is seeing – it's a TV programme, not a radio show! But what the viewer is hearing must not clash with the pictures either.

6. Let your pictures do the talking too

You don't have to write over everything, especially if emotion or beautiful pictures are happening on-screen. Let it breathe from time to time.

7. Write it to be spoken

Speak the lines to yourself as you are writing them. Try to achieve a natural rhythm.

8. Write it to link up the actuality

Try to write out of what you have just heard in the programme and into what you are about to hear. It should dovetail in nicely and link up your programme.

9. Write–improve–tweak

Keep finessing your script. Avoid repeats of the same words. Adjust the commentary as the pictures change in the edit.

10. Be colloquial

Most voiceover artists will want it to sound like their own voice – like they are saying it, not reading it. You can help by writing in a colloquial way. 'He's unhappy' rather than 'He is not happy'. Plus colloquial tends to be shorter. All good!

11. Use the 'Rule of Three'

A list of three tends to work. A list of two is too short (well, it isn't really a list, is it?) A list of four is too long. Three is great, especially for pre-break 'coming up' trails.

12. Avoid lines that your presenter can't or won't say

I once recorded voiceover with a presenter who was completely unable to say the word 'refurbish'. We got to 41 takes! In the end we got him to say 'Re', then 'Fur', then 'Bish', and edited them together. To avoid arguments at recordings, you should double-check all your facts, and don't include lines that you know the presenter will hate. Dubbing time is expensive, so you don't want to waste precious minutes bickering with your talent.

Once you have written your script, there are four things you should do before the record.

1. Choose the right voice

This is crucial. The wrong voice can ruin your programme. Recently I produced an emotional series for ITV and moved on before the voiceover was recorded. The executive, who had been brilliant in every other respect, chose a rather cold sounding voiceover artist. In my opinion, the artist was totally wrong for the series; it was a shame. These days you can listen to loads of voice samples on the internet. Choose a couple. Send them your script and get them to read a few lines to you over the phone. You will soon sense which has the right voice for your show.

2. Email the full script to the talent before the recording

Try to ensure that your voiceover artist has sight of the script and a DVD of the show in advance of the recording. This will help them think about the appropriate tone for the programme. Also, they may want to rewrite lines so that it sounds more like how they would normally say things. This is to be encouraged – as long as their line is the same length as yours!

3. Take enough copies of the script to the recording

Remember to take copies of the script for yourself, the narrator, the producer (if it is someone else) and the sound engineer.

4. Format your script so that it's easy for your talent to read

The more professional your script looks, the more secure and confident the artist will be. Don't allow one section of voiceover to split across two pages: you don't want the artist to turn pages noisily in the middle of a line. These things are easier to spot once it is printed out rather than on a computer screen. I recommend 14pt Arial font, double-spaced. It should be looseleaf with numbered pages, not stapled – and don't forget to check the spelling! Over the page is a sample of a short commentary script.

Commentary script for *(Programme Title)*

Brief description of what programme is about:

Name of voiceover artist:

Date of recording:

Notes	Commentary
On your printout of the script you can write the best takes in this column. On their printout of the script the voiceover artist can make notes in this column. What tone should this line be? More humour? Quicker read, etc?	**Comm. lines in bold below. If you have time, it's good to write the actuality or 'sync' words before and after the line of commentary. This will help you to cue the voiceover artist. It also gives them the context of the actuality into which their words need to fit. Make sure that comm. lines are double-spaced to give room for additional notes.**
Always give your commentary cues a number. Then it's easier at the end to say 'Can we do cues 3, 7, 9 and 10 again?' This column can also be used for timecodes, which makes it easier to lay back the commentary on to the final programme later.	**COMM 1** **If dogs are man's best friend – then horses come a close second.** **The bond between human and horse goes back tens of thousands of years.** **But can these intuitive creatures help people with deep-seated problems get better?**
This line is short and sweet. Name check the people, then let them talk for themselves.	**COMM 2** **Psychotherapists John and Jane think they can.**
If they can't explain it succinctly, you do it for them in commentary. This is a clunky sentence – can you make it shorter and cleaner?	**COMM 3** **John uses horses because he believes these sensitive animals can tune into his patients' emotions.** **He has found that as his patients get to know and under-stand the horses, they start to understand themselves.**

So, you have done everything you can before the voiceover recording. Now comes the fun bit!

SIX TOP TIPS

1. **Don't be scared of the red button**

   Your talent may be recording to picture: this is where they watch the programme as they read the script and say the lines. If so, you will need to press a button so that a red light appears in the voiceover booth when the recording artist needs to start each line. Don't worry, you soon get the hang of it. It's all about timing. Try to do a few lines in one go so they can get into a rhythm.

2. **Recording 'wild'**

   Top actors and actresses sometimes prefer to read direct from the script without looking at the pictures. This may be because it's quicker to do, so they can finish sooner! Recording wild is nerve-wracking for the producer. You can't be 100% certain that the commentary lines will fit into the spaces you have left for them in the cut. My tip? Record an additional, quicker read for the lines which might be tight, just in case.

3. **Record alternative versions when recording wild**

   It's always good to have options to lay back to picture – not just for speed, but also for tone and meaning. I ask for at least two reads of each line. The second read is nearly always better than the first, but don't overdo it. Read 49 may sound a bit weary!

4. **Know pronunciations in advance**

   Make sure that you know how to pronounce every word in your script. At the moment I'm writing a script where one of the contributor's names is spelt 'Johan', but pronounced 'Joanne'. The correct pronunciation needs to be noted in the script.

5. **Redo the first few lines at the end**

   It is likely that the artist's voice will be warming up when they do the first few commentary cues. Always go back and re-record the first few lines of commentary at the end when the voice over artist has got into the swing of things.

6. **Go down the pub with the talent!**

   This is your chance to get some dynamite showbiz gossip. Which Hollywood actor was so temperamental that his voice was replaced on an animated hit movie by an impressionist? Which Hollywood actress insists on someone else flushing her loo? Which star challenged his stunt double to a fight, then fired him when he lost? My lips are sealed – unless you take me down the pub!

Judicious use of these producer/director tips, along with the guidance in other sections of this book, should stand you in good stead as a producer/director. I particularly recommend that you also look at research skills in Chapter 5, shooting associate producer skills in Chapter 6 and presenter skills in the upcoming Chapter 9.

Chapter 9:
How To Be A Presenter
– And How To Work With
Them!

Chapter 9: How To Be A Presenter – And How To Work With Them!

I have had the pleasure of working with many presenters, household names and novices. Some on £30,000 for a night's work, some on much less than that. In fact the presenter on £30,000 started looking at her watch 20 minutes after arriving and asked, 'Have we finished yet?'

Most presenters are lovely to work with, but some aren't. In the former category go Lorraine Kelly, Gloria Hunniford, Lisa Rogers and Trisha Goddard. In the latter category? Well, that would be telling!

It is a tough job being a presenter. I used to have some real battles with my good friend Mark O'Shea, the wildlife presenter. I flew around the world with Mark chasing snakes and lizards for Channel 4 and Animal Planet.

I remember one heated debate on Krakatoa when he insisted on using the word 'Herpetofauna' in a piece to camera. I asked him to say 'snakes and lizards' instead – more accessible to the viewers, I thought. Mark felt that this was dumbing down. A full and frank exchange of views resulted. I think one of us might have put the other one in a headlock; it's all a bit hazy now.

There were similar 'discussions' with Mark on Guam, Saipan, New Caledonia, India, Indonesia… need I go on? However, now I look back on it, I realise the pressure that Mark was under – it was totally down to him to carry the programme. He had to find snakes and reptiles (pretty tricky), catch them (pretty dangerous), then do pieces to camera 'in the moment'. The pieces to camera were outside his comfort zone, he wasn't a trained presenter. All that is a big 'ask', so it's no wonder that he got a bit fractious from time to time. On reflection, I think he did a brilliant job in difficult conditions.

And imagine having to carry a programme which is live. You are totally reliant on the team around you. If they make a mistake, it's you who ends up looking ridiculous in front of millions of people. Say a researcher gives you inaccurate information, so you ask the wrong question, or the director leaves you desperately trying to fill airtime because a story has dropped. It's no wonder that presenters get stressed and make big demands of the people around them.

It is worth reading this chapter about presenting, even if you have no intention of appearing on camera. From a director's point of view, the more you can empathise with presenters, the more chance you have of getting a good performance out of them. It is always good to understand a rare and delicate species!

There are three main elements to presenting – the 'Holy Trinity', if you like:

1. Interviewing on camera
2. Pieces to camera
3. Recording voiceover.

Let's go through them one by one.

Interviewing on camera

22 TOP TIPS

Please note: these tips also apply to researchers, shooting associate producers and producer/directors doing interviews on camera.

1. **You need to get illuminating answers/information/controversy from your interviewee**
   It depends on the programme you are presenting, but you will need your interviewee to deliver at least one of the above. Part of your role as presenter is to help the contributor put in a good performance. The questions you ask, and the way you ask them, are crucial.

2. **Preparation is key**
   As with most TV, you cannot just turn up and do a good job. You need to think of your questions in advance, and work out your plan of action for getting the best out of the interview.

3. **Contributors need to be briefed clearly**
   The interviewee wants to come across well. You want them to come across well too. You should tell them how they can help themselves make this happen. For example, police officers often speak in dry language 'I was proceeding down the road at 31 miles per hour', and they often use three letter acronyms (TLAs), which no one outside the police service understands: 'We got to the RTC and there was an ARU there.'

   So before the interview, it is wise to ask them to imagine that they're telling the story to a mate down the pub who isn't in the police service. You want to help them come across as a human being, not a uniform. Hopefully they will buy into this and give animated, engaging answers.

4. **'Talking them up' makes all the difference**
The police pre-interview chat above is an example of 'talking up'. This is where you get your contributor into the right mental place to deliver what you want. If you are interviewing a mum whose son has gone missing, you would have a different approach. In a gentle, soothing voice you would ask her to tell you exactly how she feels, the hell she is going through as she waits for the phone to ring: 'This will increase the chance of people looking out for your son.' You might even tell her a story about a personal tragedy you've been through. You're being open with each other, it's not a one-way street. All this will help you get the emotion you need. (There are more tips on this in Chapter 6.)

5. **You may want full statement answers so the questions can be removed**
The producer/director may want to edit out your question when it comes to the final programme and just go straight to the answer. This is definitely the case if you are a researcher or shooting associate producer asking the questions. To make this possible you need to ask for full statement answers, so that they make sense without the question. For example, instead of 'It happened last year', you want: 'The car crash happened last year.' Some interviewees find this easier than others; you may need to remind them gently, if they keep forgetting.

6. **Keep the contributor sweet**
Be very nice to your interviewee as soon as you arrive. Your aim is to put them at ease and distract them while the crew gets organised. If you sit there impatiently drumming your fingers, everyone will feel uncomfortable.

7. **The 'energy in the room' is important**
If you ask the questions in an upbeat way, you're more likely to get an upbeat answer. TV likes energy and passion. If you're downbeat, you're making it harder for the interviewee to be expressive – and that's bad.

If it's an emotional interview a different tone is required. You need to be gentle and compassionate. Don't start until the mood in the room feels right and the interviewee is ready to be emotional.

8. **Eyeline**
The eyeline is the direction in which the interviewee is looking. In my opinion, an eyeline close to camera looks better as the interviewee is more 'face on' – viewers want to see faces, not profiles. Try to get your ear as close to the lens as possible. This doesn't apply if it's a two-shot interview. In which case...

9. **Position yourself and your contributor so that you're 'open' to camera**
You can help your cameraman set up quickly if you are conscious of his needs. Try to find a position which makes it easier to find a shot. If it's a two-shot interview where you and the interviewee are both in shot, angle yourself and your contributor so that you are

semi-facing the camera and semi-facing each other. It's called being 'open' to camera. Who wants to see the back of your head, or the interviewee's head?

10. Reflection technique: the long and short of it
Long questions tend to yield long answers. Short questions tend to lead to short answers. Bear this in mind when preparing your questions.

11. Ask open questions, not closed ones
Generally, you want longer answers. The reason you are interviewing someone is because you want to hear what they have to say. To make this more likely you should ask open questions:

Talk about…
Tell me about…
How did you feel when…
Tell me the story…
Describe to me...

You should **not** start your questions with:

Did you…
Were you…
Are you…

These are closed questions – someone could just answer 'Yes' or 'No', and that's useless. (The exception to this rule is current affairs, where sometimes you want a simple 'yes or no' answer from a politician – usually to land them in trouble – but they refuse to give it!)

12. Clarity is critical
Use straightforward, clear language in your question. If you do that you are more likely to get comprehensible answers.

13. Eye contact is crucial
Use your eyes to draw the interviewee in so they forget that the camera and microphone are there. It's just you and them. If you spend most of the interview looking down at your next question, you will have failed. The interviewee will think you aren't interested in what they're saying, and their eyeline will drop down to your list, so the shot won't look very good either.

Try to memorise your most important questions so that you can maintain eye contact. Have your thumb on the next question so that you can quickly find it if you need to – after they have finished their answer.

14. Listen to the answers!

Many rookies slavishly go down their list of questions and don't listen to the answers they are getting. The interviewee may say something fascinating which is begging for a follow-up question, but if you are just waiting to ask the next question on the list, you will miss the opportunity. If the mum of the missing boy says 'and his two brothers also went missing when they were his age', you really need to explore that, even if you had no idea about it beforehand.

15. The more natural, the better

Generally it is better if an interview is conversational. People are more likeable if they aren't preaching or nervously coming out with statements parrot-fashion. That being said, it's important that you follow tip number 16…

16. Don't overlap or interrupt

In conversation people overlap and interrupt all the time. You must not do that in a broadcast interview: it makes it impossible to edit the end of the answer. The interviewee also senses that you're in a hurry and comes to a rapid end when they may be about to say something really interesting. Plus it's rude to interrupt anyway!

17. The power of silence

In fact, don't just avoid overlapping, leave a healthy pause at the end of the answer. Rookies find this really hard to do. Silence is unnatural, but that's the point. The interviewee will often fill that silence with something profound, emotional or surprising. It's happened to me many times, and if you pause at the end of an emotional answer you often get tears (and in TV, we love tears).

18. Steer the interview: avoid waffle, blatant plugs and legals

You're in charge when the cameras are rolling. It's down to you to keep the interview on track. If someone goes off on a wild deviation, politely bring them back to the subject in question, and don't let them brazenly promote a product. It's also down to you to try to avoid any 'legals': libellous statements for example.

19. Don't be afraid to retake

If it isn't live and you think that you can get a better answer second time round, then go for another take. Tape is cheap.

20. Be confident

Even if this is your first presenting job, try to make it look like you've been doing it for years. TV is all about first impressions. If a big crew thinks that you're a total novice and you don't know what you're doing, they will look to get the whole embarrassing experience over with as quickly as possible. The interviewee will get nervous if they think they are in the hands of a beginner and might be offended that the production company has sent a rookie. That being said, you might want a quiet word with the cameraman, if he seems sweet, and explain that you've not done it for a while: 'Any help you give me would be much appreciated.'

21. Vox pops

These are interviews in the street: you will have seen them on local news or magazine programmes. An interviewer asks a member of the public what they think to the Budget or a new kind of sausage. The trick with vox pops is to find a good vox popee and get as many answers as you can out of them. Because most ordinary people aren't very good on camera. It's not their fault. They just aren't special like us god-like figures in TV!

22. Microphone control

If you're using a hand microphone (eg, for vox pops), keep it the same distance from your mouth as it is from the punter's mouth. And do try to point it at whichever mouth is talking. It can be very tiresome for the editor if you don't!

So those are the headlines on interviewing. Now on to another must have skill for presenters...

Pieces to camera: 'talking down the tube'

Pieces to camera, where the presenter talks straight to the camera lens, are difficult. It is an unnatural thing to do, talk to a bit of a glass as if it's a person. But if you can do it, you have the makings of a good presenter. If you can't master it – well, you're stuffed. Below are some tips on how not to be stuffed.

TEN TOP PIECE TO CAMERA TIPS FOR PRESENTERS

1. You need passion

TV loves energy and passion. If you really care about what you're saying, it's more likely the viewer will too. You need to engage the viewer to the extent that they won't reach for the remote control and switch over. When you're presenting you have to give the impression that what you're talking about is the most important thing in the world.

When I was a researcher, my first producer was Adam Hart-Davis, who is now a BBC science presenter. He used to cycle to work in a pink lycra suit and helmet. Our Head of Department, the brilliant Duncan Dallas, saw him pedal in one day and said:

'How do you fancy presenting a show about local scientists for Yorkshire TV? You can cycle around to where they come from and talk about them, doing a few experiments in the process.'

Adam jumped at the chance. A series called *Local Heroes* was born, and he was brilliant at it. That was about 20 years ago, and Adam is now a household name because he is passionate about science and transmits that to the viewer.

2. The writing is critical

A piece to camera is only as good as the script. You can have all the passion in the world, but if the script is poorly written, it won't work. If the producer who is writing the scripts has poor grammar, then you have a problem. So try to read your piece to camera scripts as soon as you can, then you will have time to rewrite if necessary. Make sure the key points stay in, but apart from that, adjust it so that it has your style. This will make it easier for you to say. Make it punchy. Use words with fewer syllables, and make sure it isn't too long.

3. You need a strong sign-off

The viewer needs to know that you're coming to the end. Then they need to realise that you've finished and something else is about to happen. The writing needs to help you with this, but so must your intonation. Don't dribble away into nothingness at the end, petering off as if you've lost the energy to present. Finish with a bang and a flourish. Imagine an exclamation mark and drive it home.

4. Autocue versus learning scripts

Autocue is where the words that the presenter needs to say magically appear on the screen but are invisible to the viewer. Most presenters prefer this approach. The alternative is learning scripts and that can be an ordeal; however, reading autocue isn't easy. The challenge is to read it and say it as if you weren't reading it.

It can be quite funny watching presenters on TV who haven't mastered autocue yet. Play the game yourself. Some presenters emphasise the wrong words, and they occasionally read a typo on the autocue as if it makes total sense: 'This weekend it will be bunny in the mouth of England.' Sometimes you can even see their eyes flicker from left to right as they read the lines on the autocue. Hilarious!

5. Look down the tube

This is the real magic of presenting. You need to look straight through the lens and through the 'tube' (the workings of the camera) all the way into someone's eyes sat at home, eating their bacon butty. The best presenters are incredibly good at this. The viewer at home begins to subliminally think that the presenter is talking to them, just them.

It's amazing if you are out and about with Trisha or Lorraine. People come up and say 'hello' as if they actually know them personally. This is because they feel they do – the presenter has been looking them in the eye for many years. Some rookie presenters just can't get the hang of this. The lens is a bit of glass on a machine and they find it hard to look at it at all. Any excuse they get, their eyeline will wander away from the lens and that all important bond with the viewer is lost. If you fall into that category, work on it quick!

6. Remember the editor!
The editor will want 'handles' either side of your piece to camera, so follow this routine:

1. Look at the lens as soon as the director says 'action'
2. Pause
3. Then start your piece to camera
4. When you finish your piece, keep looking at the lens until the director says 'cut'.

It's extremely annoying when the presenter looks away from camera to the director for approval, the moment they've finished their piece to camera. The editor wants to hold for a moment before they cut to the next sequence, but they can't because the presenter's eyeline has gone.

7. Don't be distracted
We've all seen it: people clowning around in the back of frame as a presenter tries to report on a national disaster. People also mess about in the presenter's eyeline, trying to put them off. You must totally ignore them – eventually they'll get bored. (Failing that, hire a hitman and get them 'offed' – after you've finished your piece to camera.)

8. Be yourself
The best presenters develop an on-screen persona that is an extension of what they are really like as people. Their performance draws from their real personality. From Paxman to Clarkson, Sharma to Starkey, the reason they are successful is because they're natural and at ease on camera – they aren't putting on an act. You need to be able to do the same or you'll seem wooden. Static posture and stilted delivery are achingly exposed on camera.

9. Switch on the magic when the camera is rolling
It's amazing how presenters can transform as soon as the director says 'action'. They magically switch on the charisma the microsecond the red light goes on. A good presenter can go from shouting at a researcher to charm personified at the flick of the switch – miraculous, really.

10. Express yourself!
One way of doing this is using your hands just like you would in a normal expressive conversation. Also, use a prop if possible. A camera, a mobile phone, a book – anything which allows you to converse with the viewer and feel more natural. Remember: when presenting, 'less' is never 'more', and sometimes 'more' isn't 'more' enough!

So that's interviewing and pieces to camera done and dusted. Now onto the last key presenter skill…

A PERSONAL VIEW

'Commentary' is the voiceover track on a programme which explains what is happening. It is tricky to do well. The challenge is not to make it sound 'readie' – even though obviously you are reading it. There is a lot of money to be made in being a good voiceover artist. Because you're out of vision, you don't need to be in costume or wear make-up, so you can do lots of voiceovers in a day. Get a good name (or voice) for yourself, and you can make big bucks.

I once went to Los Angeles to record the voiceover for *Stunt School* with Burt Reynolds. He dropped out at the last minute. As a former stuntman, he didn't like the concept of schools for stuntmen. It went against union practice or something. With days to go before the recording, it all became a bit of a panic, but then we found one of my favourite actors to do it, James Woods (*Once Upon a Time in America, Salvador, Casino, Shark,* etc). He was amazing. He could deliver the same line in about 20 different ways.

It was surreal saying to this Hollywood icon, 'Bit more emotion please, Jim.' 'Actually, a bit more humour.' 'Mm, on second thoughts, can you split the difference between the two?' What was even more surreal is that he wanted direction. He wanted to be told what to do, because that's what he was familiar with (oh, and he was getting $20,000 for a few hours' work, so I guess he wanted to be asked back).

RECORDING VOICEOVER: 15 TOP TIPS FOR PRESENTERS

1. **Read your script in advance**
    A voiceover artist is only as good as the script. Try to get an early view of yours. Read it. Check it makes sense. Add your style, so it feels like it is coming naturally out of your mouth, and lose any words that you can't pronounce. If you can't see the script in advance and you're reading 'cold', then get into the habit of reading ahead so that you know where your commentary line is going. If the last few words are 'and then there was a fire', you don't want to start with your 'chuckle' voice.

2. **Arrive on time**
    As with all TV roles, it's critically important that you arrive on time. If you are 100 per cent professional and a delight to work with, you have more chance of getting more work.

3. **Be careful what you eat and drink before a session**
    Don't eat garlic (voiceover booths are small). Don't drink coffee (it's smelly and induces phlegm). Resist sparkly drinks (the bubbles can continue popping in your mouth) and don't smoke (it dries out your mouth and stunts your growth).

4. **Don't blow your nose straight into the mic**
You can break the fragile membranes in the microphone. The fragile membranes in your nose may be in jeopardy too when the owner of the expensive microphone finds out you've broken his kit.

5. **Be careful what you wear**
Don't wear chunky, noisy jewellery. Don't wear a loud, ticking watch. Do have a quiet pacemaker.

6. **Don't turn your script pages noisily in the middle of a line**
For obvious reasons.

7. **Overact it!**
With commentary it is a good strategy to overact it. Then you can come down a notch if the producer wants a less animated read. It's easier to come down than go up.

8. **Try to avoid popping your 'p's**
If you are close to the mic and say 'p' straight into it, there may be a pop on the soundtrack. Aim for soft 'p's. The same also applies to other percussive letters.

9. **Recording to picture and recording 'wild'**
You may be recording to picture: this is where you watch the programme in the booth as you record your commentary. When the director is ready he pushes a switch, you see a red light and say your line. The advantage of this is that you get a feel for the programme, and the director knows your line will fit. The disadvantage is that it takes longer and is more expensive. Consequently, these days, most voiceovers are recorded 'wild', where you read a script with no picture.

10. **Express yourself through your voice**
Even though no one can see you, it helps if you act out what you are saying as this helps get more expression into your voice. The read will be better, your intonation will improve and the viewer will engage with the words more easily. Some voiceover artists stand up when they're doing their reads. Some use their hands and move their bodies as if they're performing the lines on stage. All use facial expressions to reflect the mood of what they're saying.

11. **Enunciate clearly – remember the viewer can't see your lips**
It is much harder to understand what someone is saying if you can't see their lips and observe their body language. Also, the viewer may be distracted by whatever is happening on the screen at the time (pictures, music, sound effects, etc) and whatever is happening at home (the dog eating their homework, the missus hoovering, their baby's first words, etc). When doing voiceover, your job is to overcome all this so that the viewer absorbs what you are saying. They won't be able to do this if you garble your words.

12. Pacing – take your time!

If you talk too fast, the viewer won't be able to keep up. A conversational rhythm is best, and should make it sound less 'readie'. The more it seems like you're chatting and not reading the better, but passion is still crucial. You need to be chatting energetically!

13. Voice levels – keep it steady

Try to maintain the same volume. Keeping your mouth the same distance from the mic will help.

14. Time your breathing

It helps the editor if you breathe in, pause a moment, deliver your line, then breathe out. Otherwise, they spend half their life editing out your big breaths.

15. The show must go on

As with a studio show, you will be hearing things in your ear while you're reading your lines. Take partial heed of what the director or sound engineer is saying (especially if it's 'Stop!' or 'Fire!'), but generally, just keep going. They may be discussing what to have for lunch and your input isn't required.

How to become a presenter: an insider's guide

A PERSONAL VIEW

People often ask me, 'How do I become a presenter?', and it is quite literally the million dollar question. If you do become a successful presenter you can make a lot of cash and become famous, but this does mean that there are a lot of presenter wannabes out there. The best advice I can give is as follows:

Go into TV in another role

Many presenter wannabes get into TV as a researcher or a journalist, make some contacts, hone their skills in their spare time, and then seize their chance if they get it. Jonathan Ross was a TV researcher, so was Lisa Rogers. Gloria Hunniford was a journalist and Judy Finnigan was a runner. If those roles were good enough for them, they should be good enough for you! However, beware: if you go for a job as a researcher and let slip that you really want to be a presenter, you won't get it.

Use your interests to your advantage

Are you an expert in fashion? Then do some fashion-related items for YouTube and send them off to Fashion TV. Ask about work experience or a chance to meet one of their presenters for some tips on how to make it in the industry. With so many TV channels on the box these days, there are more presenter opportunities than ever. Interested in horses? Write to Horse and Country TV. Health and Fitness? Try Body and Balance TV.

Shoot a showreel

It helps if you have a showreel to send to potential employers. (If you'd like me to do one for you, email directttvtraining@yahoo.co.uk.)

Don't be shy!

One thing all presenters need is 100 per cent confidence in their own abilities. If it's your destiny to be a presenter, then go for it – and let nothing get in your way!

Good luck – and remember the little fella when you're rich and famous!

Chapter 10:
Career Strategy

It's hard to work out a career strategy in the unpredictable world of TV. Quite often opportunities arise and setbacks happen when you least expect them, and through no conscious effort of your own.

It's a bit like a game of Snakes and Ladders. You can go up a ladder to an enhanced TV role or down a snake to unemployment as a result of fate rather than any conscious effort of your own. When it comes to climbing the TV career ladder and avoiding the snakes, luck certainly plays a part, but there are ways to make your own luck…

If your department is closed down and you are made redundant (as happened to me at YTV), this may seem like a pretty big snake, but it's how you respond to it that matters. I worked hard to find pastures new and got very lucky. A phone call out of the blue from Norwich led to a new job with some fantastic people in a lovely part of England. It was the best thing that could have happened at that stage of my career.

So, I guess the main advice that I can give you is to treat any snakes in your career as a chance to find a new ladder, and then work very hard to make it happen.

Seven top tips

1. **Be nice to everyone**
   You never know who is going to be hiring in a few years' time. He may be an irritating runner now, but who's to say he won't be future head of the BBC?

2. **Make and keep contacts**
   Good contacts are the people who may give you work, or know someone else who can, when times are hard. Treasure your contacts, and always be on the lookout for more.

3. **Be enthusiastic and fun to work with**
   People like to be around people they like to be around, if you get what I mean. If you're a joy to work with, you'll get future opportunities – assuming you're vaguely competent!

4. **Be 'absorbent'**
   Acquire knowledge whenever and wherever you can. People in TV are very generous about sharing their knowledge, if you ask in the right way at the right time.

5. **Do the hard yards and the extra hours**

   The people who progress fastest in TV are the ones who work weekends and evenings, cancel holidays if an opportunity comes up and enthusiastically volunteer for the rubbish jobs. It's a competitive industry and you need to work harder than the rest to get noticed.

6. **Don't be too ambitious too soon**

   This was a mistake I made as a youngster. I was so interested in climbing the career ladder that it became a bit of a distraction. It is better to focus on doing your existing job well. Acquire all the skills you can so that you become proficient at it. Take your time – and then, when you feel ready, start thinking about moving to the next stage.

7. **Find mentors and cultivate them**

   TV is full of successful mentor–protégé relationships. There are very few people in the higher echelons of television who don't credit their success to a close friend or colleague who has helped them along the way. If you are a researcher and you get on well with an associate producer, then stick together and work regularly as a team. Let them mentor you. Do things the way they prefer them to be done – be loyal to them, and listen to their advice. Then when they go up the career ladder, they may well take you with them. They've trained you, so they know they can rely on your work. They like you, so they enjoy your company. And they trust you, so they know you won't stab them in the back.

   This is the best strategy for getting your first associate producer credit. If your mentor becomes a producer/director and is allowed to choose their team they may well pick you. It may also lead to your first producer/director job, if your mentor becomes a series producer and gets to hire their producer/directors; and this strategy may even get you your first series producer credit, if your mentor becomes a commissioning editor and has the power to tell the production company who should run the team.

   The best way to climb the TV career ladder is rung-by-rung, behind a friend and colleague that you respect and with whom you get along.

A final message: the most important tip of all!

When you've reached the top of TV ladder, remember how much help this book gave you, and give me a job!

Best of luck!

Testimonials

Lorraine Kelly, TV presenter

Having worked with Julian on numerous productions, I can testify that he's not only a joy to work with but he's organised, utterly professional and able to think on his feet. He's cool under pressure and full of passion for the projects he undertakes. Above all, he's a grafter who knows that the harder you work in TV, strangely, the luckier you get! He has buckets of common sense and is full of practical advice. When you combine that with his creative flair, you have an incredible combination. Listen to this man!

Mark O'Shea, Wildlife TV presenter

Having had the pleasure of flying all over the world with Julian making wildlife programmes for Channel 4 and Animal Planet, I'm not surprised this book is full of amusing anecdotes and illuminating insights about how to make it in TV. There's never a dull moment when Julian is around, and he's just as funny in print as he is person. I remember once, filming in the forest at night in Indonesia, he fell down a cliff face while carrying a hurricane lantern, bouncing off every rock with his body to prevent the lantern being broken. All we could see was a light tumbling over and over, and getting further away in the darkness. Then it stopped and Julian called out, 'I'm okay!' Then he stood up, dropped the lantern and the light went out!

Mick McAvoy, TV executive

Julian has amazing knowledge of TV production. I learned a huge amount from him, from research skills all the way through to directing. He's an inspirational teacher, full of tips and advice for potential TV recruits and experienced directors alike. I will always be in his debt for what he taught me. It has become the bedrock my career has been built on – this book can do the same for you.

Bob Ottaway, former TV director of operations

When I worked with Julian he was heavily involved in training students who had no TV experience whatsoever. Julian did a fantastic job teaching them television skills. It got to the point where these trainee researchers, production coordinators, sound recordists and cameramen were doing real jobs on network programmes, and they did them well. Many are now thriving in the industry and owe a great debt of gratitude to Julian. Whether you want to work in TV, or you're an established TV professional, I can thoroughly recommend Julian's advice.

John Redshaw, TV series producer

Julian gives those he trains vast knowledge and essential skills. Today, roles in factual programming are becoming increasingly blurred. Those who continue to be successful are people who are able to multi-skill. They can find the best contributors, set up a shoot and then film them all on their own. Julian shows you how to do all that, and more. It would be easy to cram years of industry experience into a dull book. Julian has succeeded in conveying lots of advice and crucial tips in an entertaining read. If you want to understand the principles of television production from someone who will inform and inspire you – buy this book.